House Beautiful

THE
FINISHING
TOUCH

House Beautiful

THE FINISHING TOUCH

Details that Make a Room Beautiful

CAROL SPIER

HEARST BOOKS
A division of Sterling Publishing Co., Inc.

New York / London
www.sterlingpublishing.com

 33

 79

 111

Library of Congress Cataloging-in-Publication Data
Spier, Carol.
  Finishing touch : details that make a room beautiful/Carol Spier.
    p. cm.
  Includes index.
  At head of title: House beautiful.
  ISBN 978-1-58816-701-9
  1. Interior decoration. I. House beautiful. II. Title. III. Title: Details
that make a room beautiful.
  NK2115.S6448 2008
  747--dc22
                                              2008035865

10 9 8 7 6 5 4 3 2 1

Design by woolypear

Published by Hearst Books
A division of Sterling Publishing Co., Inc.
387 Park Avenue South, New York, NY 10016

House Beautiful and Hearst Books are trademarks of
Hearst Communications, Inc.

www.housebeautiful.com

For information about custom editions, special sales, premium and
corporate purchases, please contact Sterling Special Sales Department
at 800-805-5489 or specialsales@sterlingpublishing.com.

Distributed in Canada by Sterling Publishing
c/o Canadian Manda Group, 165 Dufferin Street
Toronto, Ontario, Canada M6K 3H6

Distributed in Australia by Capricorn Link (Australia) Pty. Ltd.
P.O. Box 704, Windsor, NSW 2756 Australia

Manufactured in China

Sterling ISBN 978-1-58816-701-9

CONTENTS

141

183

225

What qualities do you look for in a beautiful room?

Good design, of course, but what specifically makes a design the right one for you? Is it the style of the architecture and décor? The formality or casualness of the look? The colors? The ease with which the room can be used—its layout or equipment? The way the space relates to the garden or captures the view? Is it an emotional quality—a sense of romance, joy, relaxation, intimacy, serenity, or energy? All of these elements are important; how fortunate and exciting that they can be mixed and interpreted in myriad ways with results diverse enough to please the sensibilities of each of us.

Because everyone defines and responds to design in a personal way, there is no single iteration that is "right"—only interpretations that are right, or not right, for you. Gathered in this book are photographs of many exquisite rooms, each designed for someone with specific aesthetic taste and a pragmatic list of required components. Each photo is accompanied by a caption noting the key features that make the design appealing and successful. Look through the photos and you'll see rooms in many styles, interpreted to evoke different emotional responses and satisfy people with varied lifestyles. Allow them to speak to you on different levels—through their style, color, detail, layout, proportion, and emotional ambience, and take in the many ways they make life easier and more pleasurable. Note your responses to the décor and ideas, and as you create your own beautiful rooms, be inspired by the ones shown here that make you happiest.

FOYERS

What are the characteristics of your entryway? Does it have gracious proportions, interesting architectural details, and lovely natural light, or is it a small hall you pass through quickly? Whatever its physical features, first impressions matter. Your foyer should give your guests a sense that they've arrived at a welcoming place and also introduce them to the style and ambience of your home.

Style

Whether your entryway is a grand reception hall or an intimate foyer, imbue it with the same sense of style you give the rest of your home. Let it tell visitors that they've arrived somewhere serene, exotic, cozy, or luxurious (for example), and make it formal or casual to reflect the qualities that make you happy.

Lighting

Artificial light should be soft and pleasing, but sufficient to guide the way through the foyer and show off any furnishings it holds—overly bright or harshly illuminated entryways can seem cold or institutional. If there is a closet, be sure it is lighted. And don't neglect the exterior: you want people to be able to navigate your steps, find the bell, and, of course, admire your porch.

Furniture

The size of the foyer sets the stage for furniture: at the least, a table to hold the mail and your keys is a plus, and a chair or bench, a boon. If there's room, a sitting area with a lamp may be enticing. An accent piece such as a long case clock, pedestal, or étagère can give importance to a niche or corner.

Floor covering

A decorative rug or patterned floor immediately conveys character and can be used to define space or lead visitors to the next room (and a rug will quiet footsteps, too). When other furnishings are limited, the floor can establish an overall style.

Window treatments

If there are windows (or the door is glass), cover them, especially at night, to provide privacy.

Finishing touches

A mirror will not only let your guests primp, but it will also reflect light and make the space look larger. Artwork, both framed and freestanding, gives polish and delights the eye, and small accessories add a personal touch. Fresh flowers add life, fragrance, color, and form—enjoy them!

Preview

If other rooms are visible from the entryway, arrange them to please and entice people standing in the hall: consider common color schemes, avenues of access to artwork, the fireplace, or comfortable seating.

MIX OF STYLES

Enter this hall to a sense of wonder and welcome: the contrast of dark and light, formal and informal is delightful and seems just right for an older home that has seen style evolve over time. On the left, the mirror (which offers guests a place to primp), serpentine chest, and dressy side chairs are distinguished and stately; on the right, the checked daybed offers a more casual welcome.

CORNER ACCENT

The marbleized pedestal topped with an urn makes a charming and rather extravagant gesture at the far corner of the hall, spilling its array of greens informally against the wall.

AMENITY

With such a pretty powder room, the door at the end of the hall can be kept graciously ajar for visitors.

DRAMA

Painted all white, the architectural detail of this entry hall takes second place to the bold floor. The walls, moldings, coffered ceiling, and stairs rise serenely, anchored by the graphic, diagonal, painted black-and-white checkerboard. The foyer itself is distinguished from the hall with a different, even bolder painted pattern.

DETAILS

Elegant and solitary, gold provides the only accent to the severe black and white. The collection of intricate frames and the openwork of the bench add texture and capture the imagination. The old-fashioned black dial phone is a charmer.

AMBIENCE

Gracefully designed with a vaulted ceiling framed by arches and a staircase with a window, the entryway to this new home gently welcomes visitors to a world that seems of another time. The warm ochre hue on the walls and ceiling comes from Venetian plaster, into which the pigment is swirled rather than painted on, creating layers of nuanced color that appear softly aged.

FLOOR

The bare parquet floor adds a subtle woven pattern that shimmers in both daylight and lamplight.

LANTERN

Large and traditional in design, the lantern enhances the old-fashioned mood, glowing poetically when lighted and complementing the ebonized balusters.

PROPORTIONS

The traditional center hall in this older home is generously wide and holds a small sitting area, just right for a quiet chat or solitary read. The open stairwell effectively raises the ceiling and washes the space with light from the windows above.

INTIMATE FINISH

Formal moldings, the Oriental carpet, the lamp, sconce, artwork, and a sofa that's meant to be settled into give the space a welcoming look, as well composed as a sitting room with four walls. The sheers on the French doors at the end close the space, transforming it from passageway to room without blocking the natural light.

STRUCTURE

The stairway spilling into this entry cascades playfully in a series of wide and narrow steps that form perches for large treasures. Painted risers match the walls, keeping the structure light and calling attention to the step display.

LOCAL COLOR

The mermaid figure leaves no doubt as to the seaside locale; the island map, framed shell prints, and other ship's accoutrements complete the theme.

PERSONALITY

Furnishings chosen for interest, texture, and form impart character to this small entry hall. Essentially a passageway, it doesn't require furniture for function, but these pieces make it warm and inviting.

MIXED PROVENANCE

Old fisherman's creels on the iron stair rail, antique American geometric hooked rugs, a French buffet, and a tall clock mix happily, united by rich woody hues, texture, and great shapes handsomely silhouetted on the creamy walls.

SCALE

Moldings painted to match the white walls and high ceiling and a pale, subtly patterned stone floor bring out the simple grandeur of this spacious foyer. The few furnishings are intriguing and generously sized to hold their own in the large space; the grandly proportioned door knocker gives a similar balance to the open exterior door.

TEXTURE

The ornate candlestick, rope bench, and hexagonally patterned pillows are sculptural; with the painting, they bring tactile interest and some warm color to the austere room.

CASUAL COMFORT

Friends waiting to stroll can contemplate the countryside from the cushioned bench in this foyer—or gratefully rest here on their return. Should the weather turn inclement, the large jug can store umbrellas and the pastoral paintings will please if the elements do not.

PATTERN AND TEXTURE

While the palette is limited, varied patterns, many with dimensional or visual texture, treat the eye here: the vertical rib of beadboard wainscoting and diagonal set of the rustic tiled floor, the distressed bench with its carved and gilded back rail, the tapestry pillows with lush, heavy fringe, and the trailing foliate tone-on-tone wall stencil all contribute to an overall richness.

THEME

The love of boating enjoyed by the owners of this lakeside home is integral to the foyer design. On the stairs, large brass cleats secure the rope banister, while porthole frames hold mirrors, and a gimballed copper lantern acts as beacon at night.

CARPET

The carpet tacked to the stairs softens steps and the crisp décor, with blue and straw stripes completing the deckside look. With the risers covered as well as the treads, hasty feet won't mar the painted surfaces.

THEME

Newel posts designed to mimic lighthouses signal the proximity of water to anyone entering this home. The nautical theme is charmingly repeated with colorful floats and marine-blue cushions on the settees.

PANELING

With everything, including the floor and settees, painted white to be both shipshape and informal, and no print fabrics or artwork, the tall, paneled wainscoting brings some depth and visual interest to the space while keeping the overall effect light, simple, and open.

PALETTE

Even light colors become intense when used in volume. Here, the periwinkle carpet that spans the floor floats gently on the dark oak boards, balanced by the vast ivory space that keeps the blue from overwhelming the eye. The upholstery on the settee picks up the deeper tone of the coral-shape pattern in the carpet.

SCALE

Windows above the entryway bathe this two-story foyer in light from the nearby ocean. The grid of paneling breaks up the imposing, lofty background, while ivory paint keeps it soft in the cool sunlight.

NICE EXTRAS

The hydrangeas carry the blue hues upward, and the clear vase lets them float against the ivory walls.

SYMMETRY

With a center stair that divides into two turning flights of steps opposite the entry door, this foyer is inherently balanced. The décor uses symmetry to enhance the natural balance, with paired elements arranged in perfect opposition. The mirror carries the eye upward to reiterate the space's lofty ambience.

TEXTURE

While the walls are smooth and white, textured details interrupt the whiteness and fill it with interest: the railing is X-patterned, the worn stone slabs are laid in a grid, the stairs are covered with a coarse, natural fiber runner and flanked by rustic fluted columns, and the leaded mirror adds real and perceived dimension.

COLOR

The hydrangea bouquets are filled with splendid curves and complete the décor with an extravagant blue gesture of welcome.

BACK ENTRYWAY

Crisp, orderly, and not too proud to receive hastily abandoned playthings, this mudroom has both concealed and open storage, making temporary and long-term tidiness easy and attractive. Plus, anyone tired from sports can rest a moment and catch his or her breath on the bench.

PATTERN

The lattice pattern on the bench cushion cover mimics the inlaid diamond pattern on the floor.

CUBBIES

The search for caps, windbreakers, and sunglasses is facilitated by baskets that lift down from overhead cubbies—while you can toss things into these standing on tip-toe, they're much easier to organize or poke through than fixed cupboards with doors.

ARCHITECTURAL DETAIL

The elegant archway toward the back of the entryway frames the two windows and the carved wooden horse.

FURNISHINGS

The quirky hat rack is the first thing visitors notice when they step into this welcoming home. The hat rack and the horse imbue the space with country character, and give a hint of what might lie beyond the entry. Striped carpet leads the way up the stairs.

Eclectic

Lucky are those who possess the eye and the nerve to make magic from the miscellaneous. Take this modest entryway: a space that could so easily have been done in sober early Victorian style, it's instead full of cheerful eccentricity. Call it a foyer, sitting room, library, gallery, or stairwell, it's comfortable and lived in, not simply a passageway. Guests will certainly feel welcome here.

- The architectural details have been mellowed and made quirky by history—note the curvaceous newel post, the turning stairs that just make it past the window, the bead-board closet doors—they give the space such personality.

- A worn brick floor makes a charming segue from garden to indoors. No worries about wet shoes here.

- The bright colors are invigorating—all that sunny yellow, true blue, bold orange, and accents of jade, turquoise, red, and wood.

- The furnishings are oddly assorted but plenteous; seemingly anything works as long as it's interesting, not too large, and related by color or theme to something else.

- The lamp is a great size and shape; it sits in perfect balance with the newel post.

- The mosaic of framed pieces covering nearly every vertical inch is especially creative. The smaller pictures fit harmoniously, with no particular rhythm, on the walls above the steps, where each piece may be enjoyed when it comes level with the eye. A few more small pieces lap the under-stair molding and larger pieces hang in the sitting area; only the closet doors are unadorned.

Stylish floors

Foyers are defined spaces with an open floor plan. Whether large or small, they are perceived in their entirety, and with most of the floor unobscured, they're good candidates for a decorative floor treatment.

Wood floors can be jazzed up with stain or paint applied through a stencil or in a geometric pattern set up with masking tape. This small hallway gains importance from the graphic chevron added to its floor.

◄

A bold, simple, diagonal grid pattern always punches up the tempo. Done in quiet colors, this floor features mahogany strips inset with limestone slabs.

►

Pair a classic two-color tile pattern—such as these white hexagons offset by black squares—with some faux marble painted on the adjacent stairs. Here the reversing relationship of black to white gives each pattern distinctive weight, adding drama to the effect. ◀

A brick floor signifies country informality and adds texture and color to the décor. In addition, it's nearly impervious to wet and muddy feet. ▲

"DESIGNERS SPEAK

In every home, there's one object that makes the owners feel incredibly happy. Here some design pros reveal their favorite pieces.

"If I'm being really honest, I'd have to say my Bosch dishwasher. I have two kids and they're usually eating, and their friends are here eating, and my husband and I are constantly having friends for dinner. The dishwasher is always full, always running. Better it than me, you know?
My only regret is that I don't have two."

SHARONE EINHORN
Co-owner of Ruby Beets in Sag Harbor, New York

"A coco-de-mer. It's a giant double coconut— nutty brown, burnished, sexy, better than any Brancusi sculpture."

TOM SCHEERER *Interior Designer*

"A giant three-by-six-foot 1850s sepia-toned photograph of the Roman Forum, in its original mahogany frame. It hangs over my sofa in my living room like a giant window in Rome. It makes me dream."

PETER DUNHAM *Interior Designer*

"My silly, charming turtle mirror, which hangs in my dining room. It's a whole bunch of papier-mâché turtles that constitute the frame, and their little heads are peering into the mirror. I bought it in Paris in 1976; it always makes me smile because that was one of the best years of my life. It was Paris—what more can I tell you?"

VALERIE SMITH *Co-owner of The Monogram Shop in East Hampton, New York*

"A landscape oil painting of blue skies and green rolling hills that I bought at the Rose Bowl flea market for $50. I wouldn't sell it for all the money in the world . . . well, maybe for all the money in the world."

JONATHAN ROSEN *Interior Designer*

"I have a very feminine, very traditional Oriental rug that was my great-grandmother's. It's had five generations of feet on it. Probably not the perfect thing for our hall, but it's like all things given to us that are not our choice. Mix it with things of your own choosing, and that jumble ends up being your life."

SALLEE BENJAMIN
Co-owner of Pied Nu in New Orleans

"An antique Elizabethan box filled with letters I've received over the last twenty years."

BOBBY MCALPINE *Architect*

"I have an aloe tree at the entrance to my house. It's like a palm, but wonderfully architectural, almost cartoonlike, branching everywhere. I call it my Dr. Seuss tree."

JEAN LARETTE *Interior Designer*

"A beautiful Simon Pearce clear glass bowl filled with sand, seashells, and a conch shell that my husband proposed to me with—he put the ring in the shell. To find it, he went back to Point Dume in Malibu, where we went on our first date. Sweet, huh? I keep it on a Regency hall table surrounded by his great-grandfather's books."

RUTHIE SOMMERS *Interior Designer*

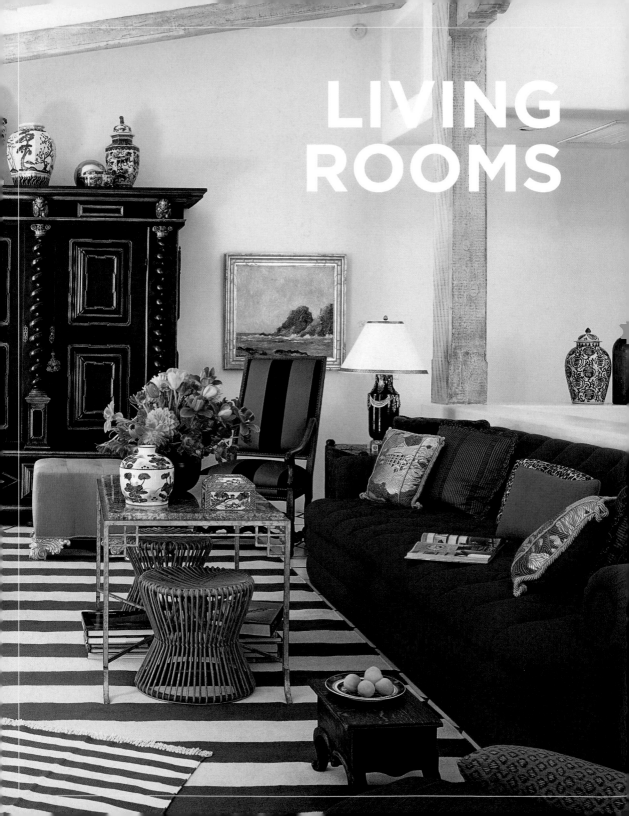

LIVING ROOMS

Where do you want to be when you're in your living room? Somewhere serene, refined, luxurious, elegant, casual, dreamy, tailored, or jazzy? Whatever the answer, you'll want the space to be comfortable, inviting, and interesting in a way that says something about you to anyone who visits.

Comfortable seating

Upholstered pieces—sofas, easy chairs, an ottoman, and a chaise or daybed if there's room—
are the pieces people gravitate toward. Consider the shape, scale, and whether you prefer pieces
that are skirted or show their legs. Don't forget pillows.

Tables

Places to put lamps, drinks, and books. A coffee table and several end tables are a must;
if the space is large, a table behind the sofa or along the wall may be desirable as well.

Furniture arrangement

Make it easy for people to converse: arrange your furniture in at least one conversation group,
placed around a coffee table or ottoman. If the room is large, set up other areas that feel more
private, for reading, taking tea, or dreaming in front of a window.

Window treatments

Style choices are myriad; whatever you select will greatly influence the overall ambience of
your room. You'll want a way to cover the windows for privacy, so if you opt for curtains that
can't be closed, supplement them with shades or blinds.

Floor covering

A carpet or rug makes a living room look finished, modulates sound, and can add color and
pattern, too. If it's not wall-to-wall, a carpet can define different areas in the room.

Lighting

Include ambient light on dimmers, reading light by way of lamps, and a chandelier or substantial
pendant lamp if it pleases you.

Accessories

Artwork and small items that are beautiful and meaningful to you will give your living room
personality. If you are not a collector by habit, don't rush—allow yourself to develop an eye
for things you love and learn to acquire and edit your possessions so that they enhance the
environment in which you wish to live.

MIX OF STYLES ▲ ►

Furnishings with varied period styles and interesting sculptural details share a palette of white with brown, gold, or rust accents to mix harmoniously against the white walls and carpet of this living room.

SEATING ARRANGEMENT

The easy chairs, sofa, and two leather-topped benches are gathered in front of the fireplace, drawn in from the walls to facilitate conversation and allow traffic to flow behind them.

ECLECTIC ACCESSORIES

Tables arranged about the room display artwork, sculptures, pottery, and other pieces that are or give the impression of being old, wearing history on their tactile surfaces.

TIP

When you're displaying accessories, if you think a single piece looks lost, group similar items—they'll have more presence in the room.

SCALE ◄ ▲

Furnishings are bold and hold their own against the massive pillars and beams and large-tile floor in this spacious room.

COLOR

Both bright and dark colors are used—along with white to match the walls—almost always separately and with considerable volume, giving each item a distinct presence and making a graphic overall composition.

MIX OF STYLES

Formal and informal contemporary and period furnishings from various parts of the world mix comfortably, unified by strong colors that bring out their statuesque qualities.

RICH DETAIL

Solid colors aside, there's something happening on nearly every piece in the room. Pattern is introduced in the pillows and ginger jars, a love of gold accents, the carved cabinet, coffee table, lamp, ottoman feet, and the elaborate mirror. Tassels, cord, turnings, moldings, and nail heads add interest.

CHALLENGING SPACE ▲ ▶

The choice of an upholstered bench to face
the sofa in this room is smart: with the area
rug, it defines the edge of the room, yet
keeps everything open because it's backless.
The bench also completes a traditional layout
where seating flanks and faces the fireplace.

TEXTURE

The soft moss and brown palette is made
even softer by the pile carpet, velvet-covered
sofa and armchairs, tufted leather on the
bench, and upholstered walls.

CLEAN LINES

Spare lines allow for upholstered seating that's generous without being overwhelming. The armchairs in the small bow window have a nice verticality that's accented by the three-legged table between them.

CARPET

A few large areas of color give the carpet more interest than a single tone would and allow the juxtaposition of moss and brown to be reversed in each half of the room.

NICE EXTRA

The easel with attached light solves the problem of hanging artwork in a small corner.

COLOR

Spring green in all its permutations graces the furnishings in this living room. From young grass greens to quiet celadons, from chartreuse to brassy moss, they're found mixed on the upholstery and rug, and echoed in the accessories. The black cabinet provides a strong contrast that's echoed by smaller black pieces.

COFFEE TABLE

Its mirrored surface reflects all the greens and creams in the room, making the large coffee table sit elegantly and quite lightly in the center of the conversation group.

CABINET

A collection of white ceramics is handsomely framed in the dark display cabinet, which sets the paler furnishings into relief and balances the darker room seen through the doorway to its right.

DRAMA

A taste for the ornate has been gloriously
indulged here: the wood furniture is elaborately carved and turned, the candle sconce
features exuberant twining foliage, and the
crimson fabrics are not just vivid—they're
sumptuous. Each accessory is finely detailed,
so the eye is engaged first by the overall
impact and again by each piece in turn.

COLOR

Red, white, dark wood—the palette is
limited, concentrated, and boldly juxtaposed; the patterned accessories feature
the same colors and, on a smaller scale,
are equally bold.

SOFA SKIRT

The upholstered pieces are contemporary
classics; intricate embroidery gives an exotic
flair to the sofa skirt.

TRADITIONAL LOOK

The high ceiling, carved moldings, and handsome mantelpiece give this room a natural grandeur that's complemented by a nearly symmetrical arrangement of formal furnishings. While the side tables, armchair, and most of the accessories are period pieces, the sofa and chairs are modern and generously cushy.

CARPET

The floral carpet provides the only pattern in the room; it makes a nice background for the furnishings and ties the dark floor to the light walls.

MIRROR

Topped by a large gilded ornament, this tall mirror fills the space above the mantel gracefully; its divided antique glass becomes an ever-changing painting.

NEW TRADITIONAL

Paired sofas face each other across the coffee table in front of the fireplace in this small sitting area. The symmetrical layout is classic and the details relaxed: the sofas are slipcovered; the large, lightly framed mirror leans against the wall; and the end tables are assorted.

COLOR

Cream, sand, and chocolate hues are rich and interesting against the pale aqua wall. The carpet provides good weight that supports the dark fireplace.

COFFEE TABLE

With clean lines and a bottom shelf, the small table between the sofas looks sharp and keeps books and magazines handy.

PROPORTION

Paneled walls bring some intimacy to the space beneath the soaring ceiling in this room; the deeper tone on the walls above the paneling also helps to define the room below. In contrast are the expansive proportions of the tall mirror above the mantel.

SEATING AREA

The fireplace is not the focus of the conversation in this room; instead it provides a background accent to the overall space, with the seating area arranged slightly to one side.

MIX OF STYLES

While the architecture of this seaside home is based on tradition, it's not overly formal and so invites a mix of casual and dressy furnishings. The plump sofa and armchair are classics with chameleon versatility, the wicker side chair and chest have clean lines and add some weight to the space, and the delicate formal armchairs are pretty and sit lightly in the middle of the room.

LAYOUT

How fortunate to have a fireplace adjacent to an ocean view; here, unobstructed appreciation of both at once is made possible by seating arranged along one wall and in the open. The raised, extending hearth carries the eye from one to the other.

MODERN AESTHETIC

An all-white palette intensifies the grand proportions of this room, with its sloping beamed ceiling, clerestory windows, stone chimney wall, and expanse of glass. The sofa, chair, and glass coffee table have style and character and hold their own within the monochrome space.

TEXTURE

The mix of smooth walls and upholstery, slick metal and glass, and dimensional brick chimney and shag rug softens the intensity of the white and distinguishes each component.

INTERIOR WINDOW ▲ ▶

A thoughtfully designed opening in the kitchen wall ensures that the cook not only stays in contact with friends, but also never loses sight of the ocean.

ROOM WITH A VIEW

Simple, comfortable furnishings that don't compete with the star attraction outside make this a room to linger in. There's not much wall space for artwork here; where there is some, the owners have chosen a tall mirror that is decorative and expands the view.

TEXTILES

Sandy tones on the furniture, at the windows, and in the rug absorb some of the bright light and add some warmth. Stripes are always right for the beach; the damask on the round-backed chair and the embroidered dark brown pillows are special choices reflecting individual taste.

ACCESSORIES

Celery vases full of shells, a large carved fish, a contemporary turned wood vase, a few flowers—what more could be needed? The wire globes overhead are whimsical candleholders.

QUIRKY CHAIR

The unusual tall chair is a wood-wing porter's chair, a form designed to provide shelter for a servant waiting by the door in the days before doorbells announced the arrival of guests.

SWEDISH STYLE ▲ ▶

Key to this look are pale, grayed colors, painted surfaces, leggy furniture, no heavy upholstery, checks and stripes, simple window treatments, plus details that are clean, simple, and edited to the essentials.

TWO SEATING AREAS ▲

Long, spacious, and flanked by a wall of French doors, this room is designed to accommodate two groups simultaneously. Matching rugs define the areas, which are separated by an antique pedestal table. One end is informal, with a sectional sofa facing a large cabinet that holds a television. In the other, more formal end, a cushioned settee and small armchairs gather round a tea table in front of a fireplace.

FIREPLACE

Flaking original paint adds to the charm of the antique fireplace surround and overmantel.

WINDOW TREATMENT

Roll-up shades are a hallmark of Swedish design; made from plain linen, these are translucent.

WALL TREATMENT

The room appears to be trimmed with moldings, but it's just deeper tones of paint that simulate wainscoting and a chair rail on the plain board walls.

LAYOUT

Defined yet fluid areas divide this large open room for various activities. Furnishings with spare lines, a shared palette, and proportions that are small relative to the space create a unified effect—it's easy to imagine the upholstered armchair being drawn from the table head to the settee or the grouping on the rug.

PATTERN

A few strong patterns dress up the simple white-and-tan palette: bold plaid cushions accent the contemporary armchairs; the fabrics on the settee and wing chair have a period flavor but are stylized and graphic, which suits the modern setting.

PENDANT LIGHTS

Dark fixtures with pale shades echo the dark and light tones of the furnishings and floor—they're handsome and don't compete with beams and skylights soaring above.

GLAMOUR

Here, gracious seating with tufted uphol-stery, a sleek glass coffee table, richly pat-terned carpet, ornate mantel and mirror, crystal chandelier, and subtly colored walls and draperies combine elegantly, without effort or pretense.

MIRROR

Over the mantel is a *trumeau*—an elaborate frame that holds a mirror and is topped by a painting—a form dating to eighteenth-century France.

NICE EXTRA

The delicate candle sconce next to the mirror is fitted with crystal drops—a lovely com-plement to the chandelier.

NEW TRADITIONAL

Windows and French doors embrace the sitting area in this room, where the fireplace is centered between two living areas. The setup is classic, but modern takes on the traditional sofa, armchairs, wing chair, and pedestal table, combined with the lacquered white coffee table and leather upholstered bench, make it very much today.

COLOR

Rich, bronzy brown walls, ragged and glazed to a high sheen and dressed with brassy tan draperies, set the white furniture into high relief. The graphic rug introduces further variations of brown, sand, tan, and cream to the mix.

STRUCTURE

Architecture is the star of the décor in this home, where exposed wood, a vaulted ceiling, stone floor, and impressive stucco chimney breast, all perfectly proportioned, frame just a few mid-century modern furnishings.

SIMPLICITY

To live simply, with minimal possessions and without clutter, was the dream of the owners of this home and suggested the use of built-in furnishings: the platform sofa hugs the wall and has an integral end table; the television sits on a built-in cupboard, one of many in the house.

PALETTE

Unfinished cedar planks line the walls, creating a background that warms the blond and cream furniture. The coffee table, designed by the architects, sits on a Lucite base like a disc of floating caramel.

NICE EXTRAS

The bronze hanger that supports the painting on the chimney breast is an exquisite detail, and the pebble lamp reminds us of the nearby beach.

SOARING ANGLES

The high sloped ceiling gives this family room a geometric feeling that is softened by the semicircular sofa and all the round elements in the room. A trio of hanging lights make their own composition and break up the expanse of the ceiling; while decorative plates and a framed bull's eye mirror over the fireplace work together to soften the hard angles in the space.

MEDIA FRIENDLY

Two televisions—and headphones—mean that everyone can watch what they want. Cartoons can be viewed on one screen while the news is being watched on the other.

FLEXIBILITY

The two ottomans by the hearth perform multiple functions: they offer concealed storage and extra seating, and the tops turn over to become trays.

CONTRAST

Dark plays against light in this open living space, concentrated in the furnishings and gradually dissipating toward the ceiling. The moldings match the walls, increasing the sense of serene space and silhouetting the dark, divided-light doors and windows they frame against the treed surroundings.

TEXTURE AND FORM

The furnishings juxtapose angular and rounded contours, textured and smooth surfaces, all in various slate hues; low backs keep the sight lines open.

AMBIENCE

Tucked beneath rough-hewn post-and-beam construction with painted plank walls, this intimate sitting area wears an air of refined rusticity. It's eclectically furnished with a Mission chair, bentwood armchair, plump contemporary love seat, and built-in painted cabinet.

CABINET

Thoughtfully detailed with simple but finely done moldings, inset doors and drawers, and open shelves—plus a contrast view of the rough roof—the cabinet displays personal treasures and opens to reveal the television.

OUTDOOR CONNECTION

A wall of windows and glass doors opens this sunny room to the garden, which in turn lends its colors to the furnishings within. The delicate chair by the window is perfect for reading, the paired armchairs and sofa are positioned to take in the garden view or the television—and all invite good conversation.

CABINET

A stylized broken pediment elevates the cabinet beyond a typical entertainment center. Creamy paint that matches the wall keeps this large piece from overshadowing the sunny space.

NICE EXTRAS

Floor pillows invite friends to drop down and relax, providing extra seating that doesn't block the garden view. The cozy throw adds a bright accent to the furnishings and anyone who uses it.

SHAPES

Furniture with square edges and a low profile introduces a horizontal element to this soaring space. The square, cut pile rug defines the sitting area; round forms—including the cylindrical pillars, lampshade, and the stylized end table and vase—punctuate the space. The leggy stools and the armless chaise keep the area open.

PALETTE

Khaki and inky green. The curtains and chaise, in deeper tones of the walls and rug, aid the dark floor in absorbing brilliant daylight.

NICE EXTRAS

Special touches here are the oxblood and rust accents that complement the greens, and the live trees that bridge the indoor/outdoor divide.

ROOM WITH A VIEW
The sandy floor of the desert seems to flow right past the massive posts that frame this expansive view, spilling onto the furniture inside.

SQUARE EDGES
Blocky modern furniture and grids everywhere—supporting the glass wall, forming the doors, bookcase, coffee table storage, and chair backs, and woven into the rug—are an orderly contrast to the wild and uncontrollable environment outside.

STATURE
The dark, subtly curved wood ceiling contains this grand room and mimics the slope of the hillside in the distance.

PROPORTION ▲ ▶

Furniture with a low profile under a lofty ceiling leaves maximum wall space for a large collection of photographs and keeps the sight lines uninterrupted from all parts of this large room. Curtains at the tall windows add a strong vertical element and balance the art on the other walls.

PATTERN

To keep the focus on the photographs, the walls are plain fields of solid color. Pattern is kept to a minimum and placed low—on the floor and on the sofa in front of the windows.

BOOKCASES

The half-height bookcases act as ledges for the artwork—the vantage point is good, and it's easy to rotate the collection.

WALL LIGHTS

Fixtures with long swing arms are centered on the walls on both sides of the fireplace to allow the most flexibility for arranging and lighting the framed photographs.

AMBIENCE

For all that the art collection holds sway here, the room is part of a home; it's not a gallery. The modern aesthetic of the furniture is a stylish and comfortable complement to the artwork.

COLOR

Dreamy tints of coral, palest taupe, and gray-blue, in varied textures and with a nearly complete absence of pattern, allow this unmistakably period room to gracefully don modern dress.

MIX OF STYLES

Curvilinear contemporary furnishings contrast with the period moldings and mantel, a modern lamp hangs from the original ceiling medallion, leather floor tiles cover the wall above the fireplace—two very different sensibilities are united by the stylishness inherent in each.

LAYOUT

The area rug supports a luxuriously cushioned conversation area centered on the ottoman in front of the fireplace; a récamier in the bay window offers solitary contemplation and is close enough to join the group.

TIP

An ottoman gives you the opportunity to do something one-off: it needn't match the chairs or sofa perfectly.

AMBIENCE

Colors that capture the quality of light from the nearby foggy sea and an uncluttered aesthetic give this intimate sitting room an offhand elegance.

WALLS

Pale, faded blue, and painted in a crosshatch pattern, the walls evoke the misty air outside.

UPHOLSTERY

Classic English upholstery, done in seafoam colors and accented with just a few floral throw pillows, offers deep-seated comfort.

NICE EXTRAS

The beveled mirror reiterates the hazy light and the intriguing architectural pillar balances the window on the opposite side of the fireplace.

CORNER WINDOW

With only a single post separating the sash at the corner, this window wraps the edge of the room with a band of daylight and offers a wide-angle view from the interior.

SEATING ARRANGEMENT

The built-in sofa places sitters flush with the sun and air; those on each side of the ell look easily across and out the other side. The two black-framed white chairs complete the conversation group but don't close it off from seating elsewhere in the open room.

COLOR

Sophisticated gray grass-cloth walls silhouette the bright window and make a serene backdrop. The pale blue sofa and shades bring the sky in through the window. The vivid yellow upholstery adds a jolt of light to the interior, reflecting the sunlight and lamps at the perimeter.

ESSENTIALS ONLY

Although quite small, this sitting room lacks for nothing as a social spot: the sofa is large enough for several sitters; the side chairs, including the one at the small desk, are close enough for conversation; and the glass coffee table is perfect for a few drinks and books.

PROPORTION

The room is long, tall, and narrow; horizontal bands of fabric on the full-length draperies introduce a sense of width instead of leading the eye right up to the ceiling.

LUXE PALETTE

Walls are finished in luxurious metallic silver and gold sheath gray, and honey-colored furnishings are accented with cream and black.

NEW ROMANTIC

Cool, watery blues mixed with sand and ivory turn sophisticated rather than beachy here: the look is calm, almost dreamy, and made modern with a shimmering wall covering, simple dressmaker details on the upholstery, a glass chandelier, Lucite coffee table, and sleek lamps.

LAMPSHADES

Identical ivory silk shades on the three lamps add a unified accent and look pretty when the light passes through them.

DAYBED

Cane ends, a plump cushion, and neat bolsters decorate the small painted daybed that sits gracefully at the open end of the conversation group.

NICE EXTRAS

Square motifs embroidered with crystal beads add sparkle to the throw pillows; tall black candlesticks add a punctuation mark to the middle of the room.

NEW ROMANTIC
Dressy, but not fussy, and alluringly reminiscent of a Parisian salon, this room is filled with petit-four colors, a mix of leggy and skirted furniture, and small collections with personal appeal.

PATTERN
Wall panels, hand-painted with a large, trailing floral repeat, and an intricate petit point carpet enclose the room with pattern, highlighting the forms of the solid-color furniture.

CONTRAST
Pure white curtains contrast the rich colors and complex patterns; Chinese tables with simple lines are a nice foil for the curvy French mantelpiece and the white *bergères* that face the sofa.

ONE SPECTACULAR ACCESSORY
The lovely antique birdcage pleases romantic sensibilities and is home to a family of white doves.

VIVID HUES ◄ ▲

Contemporary furniture with sleek, rounded shapes fills this living room with bright and citrus colors—like a large bowl of fresh fruit.

TEXTURE

Pattern is used for the background—on the multicolored rug and the variegated walls and ceiling. Solid colors, in assorted textures—soft, slubbed, and nubby on the furniture, pieced on the draperies, quilted and shiny on the pillows, shirred on the lamp shades, and made linear by the upholstery brads—play with the light to create their own, subtle designs.

OVERHEAD LAMP

The star-shaped pendant light pays a graphic, three-dimensional compliment to the motifs outlined in nail heads on the coffee table ends.

NICE EXTRAS

The cornice of hand-cut mirrors topping the cabinet, and the intricate inlaid end tables contribute to the exotic touches scattered around the room.

American Casual

Country homes today are suave and sophisticated, open and airy, well dressed but not dressed up. Rooms in contemporary homes tend to be larger, with furniture scaled up to match, mixed with things that show their history. This room has a perfect blend of elements that promise a relaxed weekend by the fire with lots of comfort and style. Here are the ingredients that make this country look new:

- The subtle, inviting colors—cream, stone, taupe, and aged greens and rust—are calming.

- A mix of contemporary and antique furnishings gives an up-to-date look. The new, traditionally styled chairs and sofa have the virtue of comfort sans the wobble of antiques; they pair well with the tables and large cupboard, which wear the charm of their history.

- The antique hooked rug grounds the décor in authentic Americana but the geometric pattern feels smart and of the moment, not sweet or quaint, as is common for the typical floral motifs.

- Varied surfaces—wax and the patina of age on the wooden furniture, upholstery that's smooth but not slick (leather) or soft but not rustic (chenille), the rug, painted wood ceiling, and irregular stone chimney— make the room warm and welcoming.

- The handsome lantern has enough weight to be commanding and is pleasantly informal, with none of the glitter of a fancy chandelier.

- One lovely painting and a few intriguing, unfussy accessories that share the palette of the room add personality and are wonderful to look at.

- The room is spacious, with the conversation area pulled away from the walls—it looks airy, relaxed, unhurried. Homeowners can stand back and take in all the details, and feel comfortable walking around to gaze through the French doors.

Focus on art

Many of us feel we're on shaky ground when it comes to displaying artwork. Relax and let the art speak for itself. Give it room, keep it balanced with the architecture and furnishings, and make sure there is light to show it off—you'll be fine. Here are some approaches to consider.

A large contemporary painting that fills an architecturally defined space may not need a frame. ▼

If you've a large empty wall and don't own a huge painting, fill the space with a group of identically framed photographs (or other graphic works with similar style) hung in a grid.

◄

Symmetry is almost always satisfying; it's natural to center the art above a piece of furniture. Accessories can be symmetrical, too, or not: if you introduce an element of asymmetry by varying the color or shape of accessories, the overall effect is often more interesting.

◄

Oversize paintings open up a room, creating a vista or second window, especially if there is no view.

►

DESIGNERS SPEAK

Some pros share thoughts about the single piece of furniture so perfect that they use it over and over.

"We always use glazed ceramic garden stools. They're great anywhere—even in showers, because they can get wet and you can put stuff on them. We especially love the turquoise ones—the glaze wavers and changes throughout."

MICHELE TROUT and HEIDI BONESTEEL *Interior Designers*

"I can't impress upon people enough the importance of an upholstered headboard. It gives you a place to recline in bed and read comfortably. It can be Louis Seize, strict and refined, or it can be a more exuberant shape, such as a camelback. In my practice, everyone gets one."

JEFFREY BILHUBER
Interior Designer

"A sofa table. What's great is that it allows you to float a sofa in the middle of a room, and it's a place to put lamps so you can free up the end tables for actual use. The only thing you need to be careful about is the height—it can't be taller than the back of your sofa, or it won't look graceful or stable."

ALEXA HAMPTON *Interior Designer*

"A classically styled secretary, usually one I design myself, often in some extraordinary color like orange or pale blue. It conveys the elegance and detail of a distinguished piece of traditional furniture while allowing for the comfortable placement of a flat-screen TV, a laptop, files, keys, stationery, takeout menus...and whatever else people need to organize. When the doors are closed, who knows?"

MARY DOUGLAS DRYSDALE
Interior Designer

"I often custom-make a 36-by-36-by-16-inch ottoman out of something very durable, like leather, and use it in lieu of a second coffee table. A large, square upholstered ottoman is a very fab thing. You can put your feet up on it and get comfortable, but you can also put a tray there, stack books, and style it."

STEVEN GAMBREL *Interior Designer*

"Orkney Island chairs. We still have them made on the Orkney Islands off the coast of Scotland. They look great in traditional interiors, and they give a modern home the softness of wood and straw."

ANTHONY BARATTA *Interior Designer*

DINING
ROOMS

Where do you wish to dine? In a formal banquet hall, quaint tavern, sophisticated nightclub, or intimate chamber? Whether you use it for every family meal or reserve it for special occasions, your dining room will give you the most pleasure if it invites your guests to linger. Consider both style and comfort as you choose the furnishings.

Table and chairs

The dining table and surrounding chairs set the tone for the room. Be they formal, casual, traditional, or avant-garde in design, they should be in scale with the room and suited to the number of diners you generally entertain. The chairs should be comfortable (antiques may look great, but fragile pieces are risky).

Sideboard

If space permits, a sideboard, buffet, stepback cupboard, or even an open area in a wall of shelves may supplement the table as a serving area or bar and offers a natural place for display.

Lighting

Chandeliers are traditional; large candelabra on the table are an alternative. Sconces add pleasant ambient light. Put the fixtures on dimmers so that you can adjust the light level (romance is nicer in shadow; clearing up and reading are no fun in the dark).

Window treatments

Include shades, blinds, or curtains that can be closed to shield your diners from passersby. If you use the room during the day, decide whether you wish to invite the sun to the table or keep it outside, and be sure to take advantage of good views.

Carpet

An area rug under the table anchors and focuses the décor and softens voices.

Accessories

Artwork will add character to your dining room. If you're inclined to maximize candlelight or a shimmering chandelier, hang one or more large mirrors to reflect the glow.

Linens

Tablecloths, napkins, and place mats in various styles offer an easy way to change the ambience to suit the occasion. Ditto for dishes, flatware, and glasses.

COLOR

This yellow surprises: it's brilliant and just a bit raw, and there's lots of it. Sunlight and reflective surfaces intensify it, as do the plum and white accents. What fun to concentrate the color, especially this color, on the floor.

BALANCE

Generous wing chairs carry the yellow from the floor toward the fabric at the window and provide visual weight that keeps the white table and chairs from floating in the space.

WINDOW TREATMENT

Perfect color and large motifs give the plain valance and drapes the importance needed to frame this dining area.

TIP

To give a room a jolt of excitement, stain a wood floor a delicious and unexpected color: moss, raspberry, tangerine. Add a few accessories in the same color family, and you have a room that's full of surprise.

COLOR

The dining area in this Scandinavian kitchen blooms with happy spring colors. The painted chairs and table share the hues of the variegated tile backsplash and the trim moldings. The seersucker chair skirts echo the effect of the pickled white floor.

CHANDELIER

This fanciful antique chandelier is draped with strings of glass beads; its graceful arms end in glass cups that hold real candles.

TILE STOVE

In the corner, a traditional tiled stove decorated with shells, scrolls, and floral motifs holds the key to the palette used in this room.

MASSIVE TABLE

A large, blocky table—a modern interpretation of a traditional farmhouse table—fills the center of this dining area; its natural wood hues match the floor. Molded white chairs on metal legs embrace it with pleasing contrast.

CURTAINS

A shaped green border frames the curtains and creates a sheer canopy at the windows.

LAMPSHADES

Above the table, pendant lamps featuring simple frames are skirted in rustic gauze. The neutral hue echoes the wood tones below; the open weave reveals the frame structure and reiterates the translucency of the curtains.

CONTRASTING LINES

The shape of this dining room necessitates a rectangular table centered between the long walls. A beamed ceiling and furnishings with stripes and curves offset the narrow proportions of the space; neutral tones keep the contrast quiet.

CURVED RATTAN CHAIRS

Round backs allow these commodious chairs to fit comfortably and seem to offer space for passing by; in addition, they add a touch of casualness to the room.

STRIPED RUG

The rug's broad stripes in soft earthy hues lead your eye back and forth across the long room and ground the honey-toned table and chairs.

SYMMETRICAL ARRANGEMENT

Identical cabinets on the end wall feature paneled doors that echo the divided lights of the French doors and bar cabinet. Between them a set of framed prints over the striped settee repeats the rectangular motif but turns it sideways.

FOCUSED DESIGN

Here, walls rich with architectural detail of another era are painted white, and the floor is polished and left bare, creating a spare background that spotlights the very contemporary dining furniture.

GLASS TABLE

The square table is glass, at once commanding and inconspicuous in its transparency.

DISTINCTIVE CHAIRS

The dark finish on their frames sets the chairs in eye-catching relief against the walls and floor, forming a curvilinear sculpture at the center of the room.

FRAMED PHOTOGRAPHS

A quartet of framed black-and-white photographs complements the restrained aesthetic of the modern décor and balances the dark tones of the floor and chairs.

DARK ACCENTS

Deep rich wood juxtaposed against a pale blue-and-white palette draws attention to the formal table at the center of this dressy room; the dark floor bordering the rug frames and balances the composition, inviting the eye to wander out and then up over the hand-painted walls.

CHANDELIER

Bridging the old-world charm of Swedish furnishings and contemporary accessories, the chandelier floats above the table like a whimsical constellation.

PAIRED SIDEBOARDS

Matching antique sideboards sit symmetrically at one end, each topped with a white lamp and centered below a mirror.

INTIMATE SCALE

A small room offers intimate dining, but a high ceiling and large window are blessings that make this space inviting rather than cramped.

CHANDELIER

This crystal sailing ship casts a fanciful light over the traditional décor—we're not in a museum.

PERIOD DÉCOR

Traditional furnishings look appropriate with the moldings in this room. The grand pedestal table and Queen Anne chairs are large for the space but work because they're the only pieces in it. Pale, damask-patterned walls, the mirror, and cream curtains create an airy effect; the fabric chosen for the slipcovers relieves the visual weight of the chairs.

TIP

If your dining space is small, use a round table—it will look lighter than a square or rectangular table and, with no corners, an extra place setting is easier to fit.

CHINESE GARDEN THEME

Orientalism sets the stage in this room: a delicate garden scene graces the end wall, fretwork armchairs sit at the table ends, the carpet texture echoes the fretwork motif, the scroll-framed mirrors reflect sprays of flowering quince, and even the cornice has a pagoda-like flare.

PAINTED CEILING

The steel-green ceiling is a lovely complement to the golds, creams, and taupes used throughout the room; with the exception of the chair seats and table, it is the darkest tone in the room and enhances the intimate and outdoor ambience.

MIRRORS

The perception of a wide expanse of natural light comes from the mirrors that flank what is really a fairly small pair of windows. The reflected branches give the illusion of an outdoor view as well.

COLOR ON THE WALLS

Here, walls painted a soft, slightly grayed shade of blue are framed by the white moldings, curtains, ceiling, and carpet, and complemented by the warm interior of the lighted cabinet and the wood hues of the table and chair legs.

DRESSED-UP CHAIRS

White slipcovers are simple but festive; they give an expectant look to the table and help the tall chairs to sit lightly against the blue walls.

TWO CHANDELIERS

Elaborate glass chandeliers turn blue or white as the walls and curtains shimmer through them. Having a pair adds balance to the dining table, which is quite long, and enhances the sense that lovely light fills the room by day and becomes magic by night.

SCALE
A small room with soaring walls, this dining area has been filled with just a few pieces, which are as large as the space permits and marked by dramatic detail.

COLOR ON THE WALLS
The walls, painted a daring hydrangea pink, are enhanced and softened with a rubbed finish. The color is a perfect mate for the blue-gray upholstery, silvery table and accessories, and statues.

CURTAINS
Although plain white, the curtains are lavish, with lush tassel fringe that echoes the turnings of the chairs and candlesticks, and the bold geometric floor.

FANCY DRESS

Brilliant green and delightful, this elaborate wallpaper transports diners to a beautiful garden. The paper provides the palette for the room, and all the furnishings except the black chairs repeat its colors—even the wood tones can be found along the branches.

FORMAL TABLE AND CHAIRS

The formal table and period chairs sit elegantly within these walls, as does the serpentine sideboard. Green velvet cushions carry the color to the table.

CHANDELIER

Tiers of arabesques festooned with crystal drops hang importantly over the table. This chandelier burns real candles and the light must dance beautifully when they are lighted.

COLOR

The brilliant sunny yellow on the walls, windows, and slipcovers dominates this room; the white ceiling, moldings, and fireplace surround sharpen its impact. It's pure color; there is no pattern except the tracery of the chair backs and candlesticks.

ACCESSORIES

A life-size classical statue draped with a harvest garland stands over the table as a perpetual hostess. The pair of lantern cage candlesticks is imposing but not dominating because dinner guests can see right through them.

PLAYFUL DESIGN

This small dining area has all the hallmarks of a formal room—wall paneling, a high ceiling, a large still life—but each is executed with a light touch and a bit of whimsy.

PALETTE

Lots of white with summery green and elegant black accents is a perfect choice for a summerhouse eating area.

PROPORTIONS

The space is small. The sisal rug defines it, the marble shelf stands in for a sideboard, the table is just the right size and, in white, seems less bulky than it is, and the wicker chairs bring a pleasing vertical to the composition.

MIX OF MATERIALS

Clean, sleek design lines allow a glass table-top, hefty wood timber base, boldly woven rope chairs, and printed cotton cushions and curtains to mix happily here.

RICH NEUTRAL COLORS

Colors reminiscent of wet and dry sand, beach grass, driftwood, and hazy sunshine evoke an island ambience.

ACCESSORIES

The wooden bead chandelier adds an appropriately informal flourish. The painting—a fragment of a painted plaster wall—sets the scene perfectly.

NEOCLASSICAL STYLE

This Swedish dining room is filled with neo-classical forms and motifs, some very formal and some softened with pale colors, as is typical of late eighteen-century Swedish furniture.

SHADES OF GOLD

Gold tones are everywhere: brilliant on the mirror ornaments, chandelier, and table accessories; mustard in the ground of the framed wallpaper panels; greenish on the table; and creamy on the chairs.

PAINTED FURNITURE

The formal lines and relief carving of the table and chairs are relaxed by soft, pretty colors. The checked pillows give a nod to the country ambience reflected in the mirror.

WALL DÉCOR

The large mirror is an imposing architectural ornament between the more delicate wallpaper panels; together, they define the seating area.

COUNTRY VERNACULAR

This dining area sits at one end of a kitchen, and most of the furnishings are country pieces from Scandinavia—a little bit dressy, softly colored, distinctive in style.

BALANCE

The doorway is off center, the tall clock and wider table and mirror nicely fill their portions of the wall space, the colors flow across the room, and one doesn't notice that the table is not centered on the doorway.

TEXTURED PATTERN

The brick floor laid in herringbone pattern is a lovely stage for the decoratively carved chairs, sideboard, and long case clock. Monochrome like the other furnishings, the wood pitcher and mirror frame add more textural detail.

BLUE AND WHITE

Dressed in classic blue and white, this dining room is perennially crisp and summery. Natural tones in the rug and window shade warm the palette.

CHANDELIER

Blue accents in the whimsical glass chandelier carry the color scheme skyward.

ROUND AND SQUARE

A large round table is a good choice for a large square space like this one—many diners can be accommodated and the open space around the table is even, which it wouldn't be were the table a large oblong. In this home, the round shape echoes the window in the gable wall above.

SUMMERHOUSE FRESH

White walls and lots of glass suffuse this dining room with sunlight by day and moonbeams at night. With this setting, accessories are beside the point.

A SINGLE MATERIAL

Walls, floor, ceiling, table, and chairs all are wood; the juxtaposition of painted and clear finishes is satisfying and the overall simplicity suits the country setting and getaway purpose of the home.

CENTERED DESIGN

The aligned interior and exterior doorways create a natural pathway, which is interrupted in a pleasing way by the dining table and chairs. From this vantage point, the rectangle is a repeating motif, moving from the French doors and windows to the table and then to the interior kitchen doorway.

GOOD BONES

Large arched doorways, a substantial mantel, and generous proportions are great features in this room; they're nicely balanced by furnishings with equally strong proportions, simple rounded lines, and subdued color.

COMFORTABLE CHAIRS

Upholstered armchairs anchor the more delicate table in the center of this room and offer an agreeable seat to every diner.

WINDOW TREATMENT

Long panels hung from rods mounted straight across the arched doorways are the same color as the walls. They're handsome but not distracting, and less fussy than panels shaped to follow the arches would be.

SCENIC WALL TREATMENT

The complex mural is a natural complement to this traditional architecture, wrapping the room with views of a distant landscape. The pilasters and egg-and-dart molding appear of a piece with the raised panel dado and boxed beams, but they're part of the faux scene.

ROUND TABLE

The magnificent round table contrasts the angular corners of the room, draws the painted landscape close, and looks intimate despite its scale.

MIXED STYLES

While at first glance this appears to be a period room, the chairs, though traditional in nature, are contemporary, as is the wrought-iron chandelier, which is gracefully accented with gold-washed glass drops.

LIMITED PALETTE

Golden toast, coffee, and antique brass hues infuse the formality of this room with a warm glow. With all the hues closely related, the monochrome background of classic architecture supports a mix of traditional and modern furnishings.

ORNATE ACCENTS

A Russian brass chandelier, the urns on the mantel, the distinctive painting, and the patterned carpet add a touch of the exotic.

CONTRASTING TEXTURES

The plush surfaces of the carpet and upholstery provide a soft contrast to the smooth table and the dimensional walls; the painting, tufted chair backs, and carpet pattern add a different, visual texture.

EXUBERANT WALLS

Walls covered with fabric printed in a large paisley pattern dominate this room, setting the stylistic tone—slightly exotic—and the emotional one—lively.

ORNATE FURNISHINGS

A grand Spanish oak table and upholstered chairs with substantial turnings look intimate in this setting. They're large, but the pattern of the paisley walls and tiled floor keeps them in balance.

EXOTIC ACCESSORIES

Primitive masks, artwork depicting far-flung locales, a mirrored sconce that reflects the action, and even the gathered raw-silk shades on the pendant lamps contribute to the sense of adventure that permeates this very individual dining area.

Beach House

Let simplicity rule at the beach: choose a home that's bathed in startling sunlight (or mysterious moonlight) and filled with sea breezes. The décor can be as uncomplicated as you like, with crisp nautical elements, sandy and sea-washed colors, or lots of white to reflect all that glorious light.

- With floor, walls, and ceiling unified in tones of soft white, this simply furnished dining alcove evokes the interior of a large seashell made pearlescent in the play of sunlight.

- The handsome, unfussy paneling, finished at picture molding height and painted in keeping with the rest of the room, gives quiet rhythm and interest to the background.

- White paint makes the board floor shipshape and pristine. Extending throughout the living area and left bare, it keeps the space open.

- Warm natural tones, obvious texture, and strong lines give prominence to the woven rush chairs. They sit in silhouette around the creamy white table, which gently fades into the background.

- The one accessory is both apt and striking—a large sailboat model moored elegantly on the sideboard.

- The shaded chandelier completes the clean aesthetic; its arms pick up the contrasting natural tones of the boat and chairs.

- The room is notable for what's not in it—no pictures or mirrors on the wall or carpet on the floor; the only textile is the white curtain fabric.

Let there be flowers on the table

Sure, a bouquet is the expected accent for the center of a dining table, but with good reason. An arrangement of flowers can introduce a shape or color that complements the overall décor, wake up a table setting that seems staid, or add a final harmonious touch. If the centerpiece will remain on the table while you dine, choose something low enough for guests to see over.

A clear glass vase accentuates the delicacy of a free-form array of roses. ▲

Spring greens and pure and creamy whites are zesty and fresh: keep the containers the color of the blossoms; add limes or green apples to give your display more impact. ▼

Purple and amethyst blooms and foliage spilling from a hidden bowl mix nicely with silvery tableware. ▲

Fill three different-size vases with a mass of single-color blooms. charming. ▼

Giant alliums grab attention in a simple setting; the organic shape of this vase is a smart choice. ▲

Choose a silver serving vessel to contain a formal arrangement; this one features flawless yellow roses, large round green leaves, and bunches of tiny grapes. ▼

DESIGNERS SPEAK

Designers know how to use neutral colors without making a room boring. Here some pros share their best tricks.

"When doing a neutral scheme, I like to use various shades of a neutral color. I also love to find old faded neutral textiles to use as pillows or a throw over the back of a chair or sofa."

BUNNY WILLIAMS *Interior Designer*

"Texture, texture, texture. I use tactile fabrics and wall coverings. In fabrics, bouclé, raw silk, natural linen, mohair. In wall coverings, I prefer silk, natural grass cloth, paper-backed linen. Don't forget the ceiling. It's the fifth wall and often overlooked—a wash of color does wonders. And art is the exclamation point that every room needs. Make a statement with art, and make it bold."

ERIC COHLER
Interior Designer

"Introduce at least one element that will draw your eye to it—a beautiful blue or ochre glass bowl or a piece of pottery. If you're afraid of committing to too much color, use a bit of exotic fabric to upholster a footstool or make a pillow. A small, colorful object like that can have a big impact."

SARA BENGUR *Interior Designer*

"There is no greater luxury than flowers. Bringing some in from the garden is a great way to add color, and interest, to a room. You can't go wrong with hydrangeas in a terra-cotta pot, orchids in a wicker basket, or even just some dahlias in an old mason jar."

TODD ROMANO *Interior Designer*

"In neutral rooms, details speak louder, so pay attention to the edges of curtains, the color of chair legs, or the skirts on upholstered pieces. Your eye is drawn to them, so do something special there. And remember, you can still play with pattern. Neutral doesn't necessarily mean no pattern. You can have a very subtly colored rug woven in geometrics or an organic motif, and it will make a strong statement."

DAVID KLEINBERG
Interior Designer

"Use a lot of different materials, in the same color. Color doesn't come only from fabrics and paint but also wood, metal, and stone. Make them all work together. And use lighting fixtures that are interesting and whimsical."

BENJAMIN NORIEGA-ORTIZ *Interior Designer*

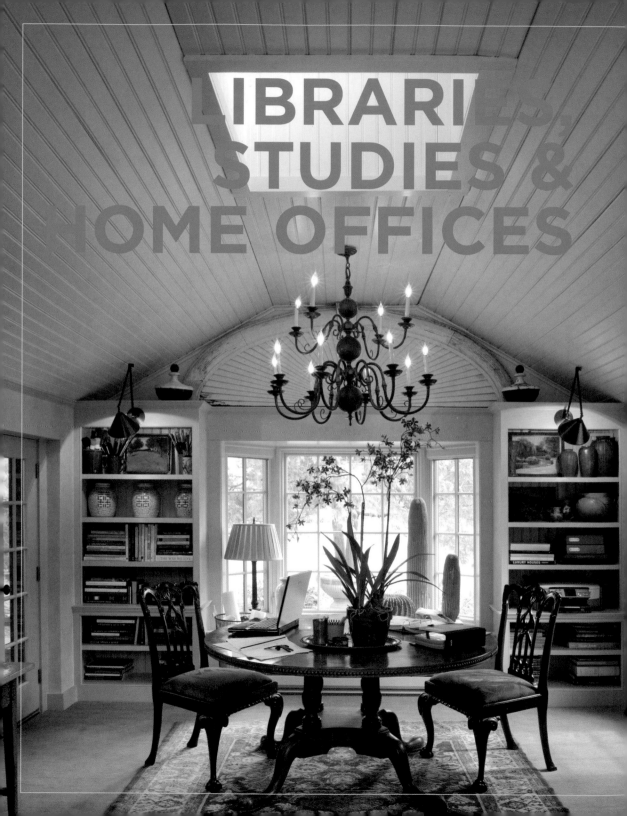

LIBRARIES, STUDIES & HOME OFFICES

Do you yearn for peaceful surroundings or wish to be in a room that sparkles with personality while you work, read, write, and contemplate the world? Do you have a room dedicated to a home office, or is your work area tucked into a corner of the family room? However you answer, create a space for working, reading, or studying that is conducive to productivity, with comfortable furnishings and a décor that makes you happy.

Furniture

A desk or writing table with a comfortable chair is essential. Choose a style that looks professional and smart, or something more in keeping with the rest of your décor, as makes sense for the way you use the space. If there is room, add a sofa and easy chair, along with a coffee table, so you can enjoy company, a good read, or a nap.

Storage

Incorporate cabinets and bookshelves that facilitate the way you use your office or library. Built-ins may be an efficient and great-looking option that you can design to truly suit your taste and needs.

Lighting

Task lighting will keep you focused—choose classic table lamps or something more industrial in style. Library lamps or built-in fixtures are nice for bookcase walls.

Window treatments

Go for a style that suits the aesthetic of your room—but whatever that may be, include something that filters sunlight away from your computer screen, darkens the room for video if necessary, and provides nighttime privacy.

Floor covering

A rug or a carpet will modulate distracting noise, but just as important, it will make your library or office look pulled together and finished.

Accessories

If you need desk accessories, there are all manner of ingenious devices to choose from. Artwork adds sophistication, poise, and may be your muse. Vases, throw pillows, and collectibles will reflect your personality and make you smile.

AMBIENCE ▲ ▶

Poised and professional, this home office reflects the taste and passion of its owner: fashion is her subject; good design, her rule. The décor is tailored, interestingly assorted, and kept tidy with stylish accessories.

PALETTE

A background of golden hues makes the space warm; accents in apple green, white, and black give it orderly flair. Note the striped ceiling.

FURNISHINGS

A big round pedestal table serves as consultation center for visiting clients and doubles as desk for a laptop computer. An L-shaped bank of lateral files provides ample storage and useful counter space and leaves the walls clear for artwork, while modular shelves display reference books, photos, and more storage accessories.

NICE EXTRAS

The smart, glen plaid–covered memo board, and the thin stainless counter that floats discreetly on top of the files add polish here.

REFERENCE ROOM

This diminutive research area reflects the interests of an art collector who loves texture, pattern, and handmade objects: the unique table and chairs and scroll-patterned rug are as much part of the display as they are serviceable; sculptural objects mix with essential books and a little bit of kitsch.

BOOKSHELVES

Shelves divided into a grid of compartments are easy to organize; painted white, they nearly disappear against the walls, so their contents create a backdrop of informal texture and pattern.

AMBIENCE

Sliding shoji screens, grass cloth covering the walls and ceiling, and a lacquered trunk give this home office a tranquil aesthetic that's complemented by the spare lines of the other furnishings and enhanced by the natural palette.

DESK

Contrasting wood colors create a framework for the built-in desk that echoes the grid of the screens. Beautifully designed, the unit includes stepped back shelves inset above the desk counter, overhead lights, and cupboards and drawers.

TEXTURE

The textured walls and carpet and the linen cushion and pillow on the daybed add a gentle contrast to the sheen of the polished wood, trunk, and leather seating, softening the geometry of the design without adding pattern and deepening the peaceful, quiet mood of the space.

AMBIENCE

The informal office area in this old-garage-turned-artist's-studio champions the eclectic: an antique table serves as a desk, an aged mantel propped against one wall bestows history where none exists and emulates a traditional sitting-room focal point, and bold striped curtains dress the windows in circus whimsy.

MIX OF STYLES

The accessories reflect a love of old and exotic objects, ranging from an ornate gold frame to a primitive mask. The owner confesses to a lamp fetish, indulged here with two modern Tizio desk lamps and an antique turquoise glass oil lamp.

NICE EXTRA

The classic corkboard behind the desk is nothing fancy, but it fits the space and works perfectly to host a constantly changing collection of clippings.

NEW TRADITIONAL

Ladylike in pink and taupe, this office area features two classic bookcases on cupboards, trimmed with the same crown molding that frames the walls and separated by a wide shelf over a drawer. The desk is simply a glass slab set on sleek metal sawhorses; it's paired with an elegant wooden swivel armchair on wheels.

COLOR

The pink bookcase interior is a pretty surprise, lending a feminine finish to the white architectural storage and sober taupe walls and tying the sofa and rug to the office area. The lamp and vases complete the picture.

NICE EXTRA

The generous crisscross ribbon memo board between the bookcases dresses up a personal collage of beloved photos.

OFFICE TEMP

This rustic screened porch shelters a summer office—unless brisk winds blow damp weather onto the desk, in which case portable electronics, books, and casually displayed artwork can be quickly gathered and taken indoors.

AMBIENCE

Inherently charming and casual, the brick-floored gingerbread structure is made more so by candlelit fixtures, a hanging vase filled with fresh flowers, the sawbuck table and bistro chair that symbolize a place of business, and assorted accessories chosen for personal inspiration.

NEW TRADITIONAL

Formal architecture with ornate pilasters
and moldings frames inset shelves in this
spacious and elegant library, where family
can gather to solve jigsaws and debate the
news, or sit apart to read quietly.

READING ROOM

A reader can be comfortable in a variety of
settings here—sitting upright at the round
table or in the armchair, or reclining before
the fire on one of the chaises.

WINDOW TREATMENT

A cloud shade raised high in the window
adds a pretty gesture to the décor—
it's dressy but generous rather than crisply
formal, and repeats the gold hue used for
the armchair, frame, and sconces.

MIX OF STYLES

Informal but definitely pulled together, this office happily blends the high wainscoting typical of Arts and Crafts architecture with more modern built-in shelves and desk. The rope-laced desk chair looks businesslike but shares the casual aesthetic of the rattan armchair, mattress-cushioned sofa, and plantation shutters that filter the light.

FABRICS

Simple cotton fabrics, both striped and solid-color, cover the sofa, cushions, and throw pillows, giving a summer-porch welcome to visitors. Rustic raw silk panels in the wainscoting introduce some soft texture, complement the rattan and rope, and reinforce the casual ambience.

NICE EXTRAS

The faux-marble painted on the wide board floor, and the grand crown molding topping the shelves are elegant finishing touches.

UNDER THE EAVES
Tucked between low knee walls under sloping ceilings, this office enjoys the magic solitude of an attic retreat. Simple furnishings fit the space neatly.

NICE EXTRA
The wheeled cabinet in the corner, pulls out to prevent head-bumping during lengthy filing sessions.

TAILORED
Striped wallpaper on the gable wall brings a serious but lively focus to the room and establishes the brown, white, and blond palette. The furnishings are handsome, tailored, and small in scale, as befits the proportions of the space, and though not strictly symmetrical, the layout is balanced.

FLOATING
The Lucite table base and chair disappear, enhancing the open, uncluttered look.

LUXURY OF SPACE
Grand proportions, traditional architecture with French doors opening to a terrace, elegant furnishings, and a tranquil cream and brown palette make this combined office/sitting room a retreat to envy.

MIX OF STYLES
Each piece in the room is beautiful and interesting in itself and in contrast to the others, with the desk and *bergère* honoring tradition and the sitting area reflecting a more modern aesthetic.

CHANDELIER
The glass chandelier is gracious and not at all fussy, topping off the décor with a pretty flourish.

ROOM TO READ

With one wall lined floor to ceiling with
open and closed shelves, this modern library
in a city apartment stylishly fulfills the fun-
damental purpose of a library: a comfortable
place to store and read books. The warm
color palette makes this room an especially
inviting place to recline and read. A few
decorative objects are perched among the
books, breaking up the expanse of spines.

AMPLE SEATING

A commodious sofa, along with two additional chairs, is the perfect place to read
or sit with guests and watch a movie on the
television that's hidden behind the panel.
The built-in bench under the window is a
nice extra.

ESSENTIALS

A desk, a chair, and good lighting are all you need to create a functional study. Here are those three basics and more, all working together with panache. The blue leather chair is a throne fit for a king—comfortable, stylish, and classic. The color is striking, and the nail heads emphasize the chair's curvy lines. The lamp and window throw plenty of light onto the task at hand, whether it's writing a letter or paying bills.

COLOR

Shades of blue appear throughout the room, from the desk accessories to the flowerpots to the blue bottles (part of a collection) atop the glass-front cabinet. The chocolate-brown walls infuse the space with a touch of formality, and is a classic pairing with blue.

DETAILS

Decorative objects abound throughout the space, adding a personal touch and giving the room plenty of ambience.

EASY LUXURY

Half-paneled walls, casement windows with arched sash, and an Oriental rug provide an orderly backdrop to the modern furnishings in this small office. The leather-upholstered chairs are sleek, luxe, and understated; the desk is visually light and accessible from both sides, like a restrained interpretation of a partners' desk.

COLOR

Taupe, gold, and mahogany tones, with black accents, make this room masculine and warm; the small proportions and dark walls invite contemplative work or relaxation.

IN THE STACKS

In an excellent use of an interior hallway, bookshelves extending from the baseboard to the ceiling keep a small library in easy reach of bedrooms; they're handsomely built-in, with their fronts flush with the wall.

ACCESS

Books on the top shelves can be reached via a small stepladder; anyone wanting to sit and browse a volume can flip the ladder top down to transform it into a chair.

LIGHTING

A library lamp mounted above each stack of shelves illuminates the titles; a small, dressy, brass chandelier with mesh shades sheds a gentle glow overall and complements the papered raised ceiling.

HOME STUDY

A rustic trestle table acts as desk for a couple who bring their laptops to this study on weekends. Antique rush-seat armchairs cushioned with big pillows provide comfy seating. Anyone wanting to escape with a good book heads to the wing chair and puts his feet up on the ottoman.

WALLS

Board paneling, narrow and vertical above the windows, wider and horizontal below, wraps the room. Painted khaki green and dressed with matching tattersal drapes, it's cozy, quiet, and serene. A series of botanical prints adds a uniform embellishment.

RUG

An unusually large example, the geometric American antique hooked rug softens and relaxes the décor with informal, folk art charm.

AMBIENCE

Warm colors, walls lined with books, and a large sectional sofa placed right against the bookshelves make this a spot to settle into for relaxing, reading, and good conversation.

WINDOW TREATMENT

The valance, scalloped across the center and with long sides, gives a sense of intimacy without closing off the daylight. This style, sometimes called a lambrequin, lends a touch of formality.

PATTERN

Happily defying the conventional wisdom that patterns should differ in scale within a room, both the sofa and rug are boldly figured—the color balance is so different on each that the mix works. The crisscross bookshelf ends and a few solids and stripes accent the effect, with everything set against walls lightly textured by herringbone upholstery.

TOGETHER OR APART

Two steps lead from this friendly sitting area to a private reading nook that's fitted with a thickly cushioned window seat, plump pillows to rest against, a set of shelves for must-read titles, a good light, and a view to dream over.

PALETTE

Cream, sepia, sand, deep leather-brown, and a seasoning of terra-cotta communicate a relaxed, old-fashioned comfort that's perfect for the seaside or any country home.

WALLS

Built-in cupboards—some open and some closed with paneled doors—line the sitting room walls. Above them, and in the reading nook, cream walls ragged with sand-color paint have a soft, irregular finish that mimics the play of light and water on the nearby beach.

WOODWORK ◄ ▲

Complex traditional molding with paneling
dominates this small library. It frames the
bookcases, trims the arched doorway,
surrounds the fireplace, tops the walls, and
fronts the base of the banquette in the bay
window across from the sofa.

AMBIENCE

The irregular shape, large fireplace, dark
brown woodwork, and moss green walls
seem studious and cozy; they're offset by
white carpet, red and white fabrics, and the
natural light spilling through the window.

WINDOW SEAT

A high back, thick cushions, and soft throw
pillows guarantee a comfortable read on
this window seat. The windowsill extends
to top the back with a shelf that displays
photos and will gladly hold a cup of tea.
Lamps with swing arms provide light when
the shades are down.

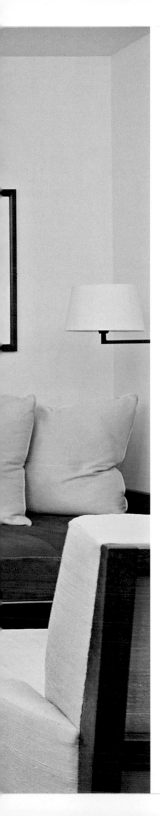

Modern

If we're going modern, we'll look for sleek lines, graphic qualities, and comfort grounded by a bit of austerity that quiets, soothes, and clears the mind. The look needn't be angular—clean curves are welcome. Colors can be vivid or muted, and varied by slick surfaces or soft textures. We love the clean simplicity of this study.

- Sleek, low, and framed with hard edges, the furnishings are nonetheless invitingly soft, with firmly stuffed cushions and plump throw pillows.

- Cream, gold, olive, and terra-cotta hues give a warm cast to the white room; there is no pattern and the effect is quiet, nuanced, and sophisticated. Subtly textured fabrics and a mohair rug add to the soft contrast.

- We like the way the dark floor makes a frame between the walls and center of the room, adding another graphic and linear element to complement the furniture.

- The small wrought-iron and wood desk, and the lamp on top, are not at all office-like. They were designed early in the twentieth century by French architect Pierre Chareau; a testament to enduring design, they still look modern and the desk is still in production.

- The uncluttered look is enhanced by the cushioned ottoman at the desk: there is no chair back adding a vertical element, and the ottoman is easy to pull out to position near the sofas.

- The floor lamps are simple and graphic, with white shades that nearly disappear. The subtle asymmetry in their height and the off-center placement of the art are intriguing.

Kick back with a good book

Indulge yourself by outfitting your library, office, or study with one piece of wonderfully comfortable seating—the type that lifts your feet off the ground—so that when it's time to relax with the paper or an engrossing book, you can truly settle back and concentrate. Naps are okay, too.

A chaise with two upholstered arms gives plenty of support to bent elbows so hands can hold the newspaper upright. The back on this one has very little incline, which may encourage you to stay awake. ▼

A plump upholstered easy chair with a matching ottoman looks tailored in a more formal setting. Move the ottoman aside when you wish to appear dignified; pull it up to the chair for your feet when relaxation is in order. ▲

A classic armless chaise works as a bench as well as a recliner: you can perch on either side to join others in conversation, or stretch out for a solitary read. ▼

If the clean lines of modern furniture suit your style, choose something like this zigzag-shape chair—neither recliner nor chaise, it has the advantages of both. ▲

Libraries and studies don't have to be the exclusive domain of chairs. Nail heads add a masculine touch to this plush paisley-covered sofa situated in a quiet study. ▼

Whether to prop up feet or serve as a seat, a pillow-topped ottoman is extra inviting. ▲

DESIGNERS SPEAK

Asked what touches can be added to give a room heart and soul, experts offer these suggestions.

"Objects imbued with memories. In my parents' vacation house, there are old rods and reels; a propeller from a boat we used to own; a beautiful model sailboat that my dad helped me build when I was ten; and my mom's collection of 1930s green-and-white plates, which have been hanging on the same wall forever."

JAN LEE *Furniture Gallery Owner*

"Family photographs, a dog, and a sofa you can vacuum."

KITTY HAWKS *Interior Designer*

"Evidence of life. Anything from children's art to dog-eared magazines to fresh-cut flowers that aren't perfect."

RACHEL ASHWELL *Founder of Shabby Chic*

"Books. They're intimate and revealing. My very first client was a great reader, and she had this magnificent library with thousands of books in vertical stacks. Some were used as stands. Some were used as tables. Nothing was arranged properly. It was amazing."

PAUL VINCENT WISEMAN *Interior Designer*

"Good old Oriental rugs give a beautiful soul to a room."

MONA HAJJ *Interior Designer*

"Using a room gives it heart and soul. People never use their living rooms. You've got to take it back, give it another purpose rather than just entertaining. Put your easel or drafting table in it like Jackie O did. Put your computer in it. Or put a big double-wide wicker chaise longue next to the fireplace with a big mohair blanket at the end and make it your prime napping spot.

TOM SCHEERER *Interior Designer*

"Red rooms always have heart and soul."

MARY MCDONALD *Interior Designer*

"All those subliminal things you don't really see but experience, like solid wood doors with solid brass hardware. And there's nothing like *real* hardwood floors—that lovely creak."

MAUREEN FOOTER *Interior Designer*

KITCHENS

How do you describe your dream kitchen? Is it a warm, old-fashioned room or one that shines with crisp modernity? Is it all white, all wood, all stainless steel, cheerfully colorful, or some unique mix? Is your actual kitchen large enough to be a hangout for friends and family, perhaps open to another room, or is it a small space where you work solo? Whatever the ambience you yearn for, consider the following as you plan.

Occupants

The number of cooks and whether children and guests are likely to hang out in the room should be considered from the beginning of any kitchen design.

Layout

Key to efficiency and the pleasure you'll get from working in the room is the arrangement of appliances, sink, and work surfaces. The goal is to minimize the amount of walking required and maximize the amount of work surface and storage. If the concept of a work triangle leaves your eyes glazed, get help from a professional kitchen designer.

Surfaces

Materials make a statement: wood, painted finishes, stone and man-made look-alikes, stainless steel and other metals, glazed tiles, laminates, glass, even concrete—each has its place in the kitchen. Decide which of them belong in yours as you choose cabinets, countertops, appliances, and flooring, and in what color if there are options. Make sure you understand how to care for your chosen materials.

Storage

Adequate storage means your kitchen counters are free of clutter and ready for work. Open storage can be very appealing, as long as the items stored are nice to look at and neatly arranged. Bottom cabinets and islands supply a work surface as well as storage, so think about both functions when deciding how many you need. A pantry is a boon if you've room.

Lighting

General light should be even and preferably on dimmers. Install task lighting where it's needed—over the sink, stove, and work areas. Fixture options are myriad, and many have flexible mounts so that they can be focused exactly where needed. Exhaust hoods often incorporate lights. Daylight is a plus to the overall ambience.

Flooring

Choose it for its aesthetic qualities, but consider what it will be like to stand on and how it will stand up to spills and foot traffic. You might want to consider different materials for different areas.

MIX OF OLD AND NEW ▲ ►

A comfortable country kitchen with a traditional aesthetic, this room features totally up-to-date appliances, a top-mounted apron sink, recycled marble and wood counters, and all sorts of retro-style and vintage accessories that complete its nostalgic appeal.

CABINETS

Designed to replicate a traditional English butler's pantry, the new cabinets have flat-front drawers over paneled doors—simple and comfortably familiar. The hardware is a mix of bin pulls and English cupboard latches, distressed with sandpaper so it doesn't look new.

BACKSPLASH

Classic white subway tile, installed five-feet high for an old-fashioned look, provides ample protection from splashes and splatters and makes an uncomplicated backdrop for colorful crockery.

PANTRY WALL

A pantry wall that includes the refrigerator as well as a glass-door cabinet filled with transferware and charming marmalade tubs is separated from the prep area by a surprisingly formal table and chairs.

CHALKBOARD DOORS

Schedules and shopping lists are easy to monitor when a blackboard surface is added to cabinets; anyone who can't cook can practice her drawing, too.

AMBIENCE

A minimalist aesthetic reigns in this loftlike space, which features a high ceiling and board walls painted white. The flush doors set in the wall behind the farm table conceal the refrigerator; the stainless appliances and simple cabinets merge into the adjacent wall. Nothing decorates the walls.

WORKTABLES

Two tables—one wood and one metal— lightly stand in for islands. They're in keeping with the spare, open look and offer plenty of work surface (or a place to display fresh artichokes—still on their stems on the farm table, ready to cook on the metal one).

STORAGE

A bank of simple white cabinets set into a recess next to the oven provides concealed storage, as does a closet next to the refrigerator. The open shelves above the cabinets are nicely proportioned for the tall room; the stainless counter and backsplash visually recede and complement the appliances and the worktable.

JAZZY LOOK

Simple lines and an interesting play of levels
have an understated modern aesthetic; cool
pendant lights and striking bright red chairs
raise the tempo.

SHELF LIFE

Open shelves give a graphic finish to the
back wall of this kitchen. While they match
the cabinets, they're visually lighter than
the expected upper storage units, provide
space for restrained display, and are nicely
offset next to the shelf on the range backsplash and the hood. Note the deep wood
backsplash on the countertops –perfect for
storing condiments.

ISLAND

The small island is just deep enough to hold
the stainless double sink, which is integral
with its countertop; the remainder of the
island and the attached table are topped by
stone, as are the other cabinets. Since the
tabletop is dropped to standard height below
the island, snackers sit comfortably on chairs
instead of stools.

TIP

*Forego upper cabinets if you want your kitchen
especially light and airy—if you can afford to
give up the storage space they provide.*

COLOR ▲ ▶

Brilliant white seaside light floods through
the doors and windows and bounces off the
walls and ceilings in this large eat-in kitchen;
the rich wood tones of the floor, cabinets,
island, table, chairs, and hutch keep the effect
sunny but absorb some of the glare.

HUTCH

The large cabinet on the far wall of the eating
area most likely comes from an old dry
goods store or a library. Its sliding glass
doors show off a collection of white dishes
and crockery. Topped with a surfboard, it
has great presence and the right heft to balance the work area on the opposite side of
the room.

ISLAND

A worktable with stature to match its setting, this rustic island has a mix of drawers
and open shelves. It's been plumbed, too,
with two sinks, and topped with a white
marble slab. The near sink is accessed from
the stove side and features a faucet with a
long, flexible neck. The far sink is accessed
from the eating-table side.

ISLANDS

Twin islands facilitate efficient work in a square kitchen area, allowing the cook to pivot between their parallel work surfaces. Here a farmhouse sink is dropped into the back of the near island; behind it is an auxiliary oven. A commercial-style range is just a few steps away.

FLOOR

White tiles with black square insets form a classic country pattern underfoot; the bold scale anchors the chunky cabinets.

ACCENTS

Brass cabinet hardware, faucet, and lamp frames combine with white marble countertops, blue check lamp shades, blue glassware, and blue enamel cookware to add a dressy finish to this hardworking space—a nice segue to the formal mirrored china cabinet and pretty cane-back stools.

LAYOUT

There's no danger of bumping elbows in this commodious kitchen, which happily accommodates multiple cooks and any family and guests who want to hang out. A grand bow window thrusts lots of work space into the sunlight and invites ambient rays into the interior as well. The generous island in the middle of the room puts additional work surface and storage within just a few steps of the range, refrigerator, and sink.

MIX OF MATERIALS

The array of stainless steel; white cabinetry, walls, and ceiling; glass; black marble; and butcher block creates a professional ambience that invites you to don an apron and get busy. The tile floor, laid in a hexagonal dot flower pattern, adds a soft visual to the crisp utilitarian space. Antique glass pendant lights cast a warm glow.

REFRIGERATOR

The pass-through refrigerator, designed for restaurant use, keeps cold things visible and accessible from the kitchen and the adjacent room as well.

SURFACES

A mixture of silvery bright stainless and charcoal brushed steel, blue enamel, and rustic wood painted red gives this state-of-the-art kitchen a comfortable country ambience.

STOVE WALL

An expanse of stainless steel covers the wall between upper and lower cabinets, stove and exhaust hood with professional élan. The attached shelves and utensil racks are no-nonsense and great-looking.

NICE EXTRA

The window at the sink is slightly recessed and sits several inches above the counter; its sill makes a handy shelf for stashing small treasures or ripening vegetables.

LAYOUT

Fitting sleekly in an open-plan living area, this kitchen is perfect for the cook who likes company while preparing a feast. There's plenty of room for visitors to hang out, with lots of counter space for those who wish to help.

CABINETS

All white, with clean lines, stainless pulls that complement the appliances, and white marble countertops, the cabinets are handsome yet unobtrusive in the open space. Glass doors on the upper units echo the windows on other walls.

ISLAND

The thoughtfully designed island features a seating area with trendy stools, framed at each end by a cabinet. Drawers that open to the adjacent dining area are handy for flatware, place mats, and linens. The small prep sink supplements another, large one, not visible here but to the left in the opposite counter.

LAYOUT ◄ ▲

The layout of this U-shaped kitchen is super-efficient. It has lots of counter and cabinet space, a large sink, and a commercial cooktop plus wall oven and microwave—all in an apartment where space is at a premium.

MATERIALS

The industrial look of stainless steel and black granite is warmed by cherrywood. The horizontal board doors on the cabinets are spare and modern.

SNACK BAR

Cantilevered on steel brackets and raised higher than the kitchen work surface, the granite counter adjacent to the sink sits lightly, seemingly floating.

NICE EXTRAS

Bars on the stainless stove-wall backsplash support utensils and small hanging shelves. A tambour door on the upper cabinet at the closed end of the work area slides up to reveal small appliances and storage compartments, and slides down as a sleek façade.

TIP

A bottom-drawer freezer saves wear on your back because you access the freezer less frequently than the vegetable drawers in the refrigerator.

AMBIENCE ▲ ▶

Wood cabinets in the Arts and Crafts style, matchstick Roman shades, and sedate tiled walls pair with sleek appliances, slate countertops and floor, and very contemporary stools, table, and chairs to make this eat-in kitchen at once warm, low-key, and of the moment. The rug carries the warm wood tones of the cabinets to the eating area.

LAYOUT

This room is easy and efficient to work in— the sink and cooktop are opposite and close to each other and centered between the ovens and refrigerator. There's lots of counter space, with sunlight from the paired windows and recessed skylight reaching most of it.

NICE EXTRAS

A spigot in the backsplash behind the cooktop means large pans can be filled with water when they're on the burner instead of being carried from the sink. The hood includes a pot rack—handy and handsome.

FOCUS ON DAYLIGHT

A long narrow kitchen in an urban home, this room refuses to be dark or cramped. The tall French door at the end lets in lots of light (and opens to an intimate, church garden view). With daring, the designer of this space placed a bank of lower cabinets and the commercial cooktop in front of a window; the view is reflected in the glass doors of the opposite cabinets. Making a neat display and enhancing the passage of daylight, the tall cabinet to the right of the door is glass on two sides.

NICE EXTRA

Because the ceiling is so high, there's room for more upper cabinets than is usual. The metal bar running between the two tiers on the left supports a rolling ladder.

TIP

Pay extra attention to the little details. Make sure the doorknobs, cabinet pulls, lampshades, and accessories are special.

COLOR

Classic country-style cabinets in deep charcoal demonstrate that dark color needn't translate to gloomy. Here, the dark is balanced by light walls, ceiling, and floor. Glass doors on the upper cabinets add to the open effect, as does the fact that the work area opens to living space on one side.

ISLANDS

In any kitchen, an island supplements storage and work space; in this long area, two islands do that better than one, allowing easy access to the counter and appliances on the exterior wall. The island sink is accessed from the open room side to allow the refrigerator door behind it to swing open when someone is washing vegetables.

GRAPHIC DESIGN

Clean lines and a restrained palette punctuated by carefully introduced spots of color give this well-appointed kitchen a crisp but welcoming demeanor. The only pattern is monochrome and linear: lattice backs on the stools, tiny rectangular tiles on the walls, upper cabinet symmetry, and horizontal folds on the window shade.

ISLAND

This roomy kitchen easily accommodates a large island, which provides a transitional work space in the L-shape layout and beckons to friends in the adjoining dining area. The small prep sink placed at the end farthest from the big farmhouse sink is handy for activities to the right of the stove and leaves most of the island free for work or breakfast.

LAYOUT

The basic galley layout places the cleanup area with a large sink and two dishwashers on one side, and command central for cooking on the opposite wall, with a huge range, prep sink, and tall cabinets that conceal a refrigerator and freezer. The enormous, counter-height table in between serves as workstation and snack bar.

SCALE

Generous proportions, windows on three sides, and top-notch equipment make this kitchen ideal for serious cooking, with guests and family welcome to help or hang out. White marble topping dark legs creates a dramatic central island that appears to float above the ebonized floors.

MIX OF MATERIALS

A mix of pure white and stainless steel looks dairy-clean and streamlined above the dark floor. The stainless countertops are welded, not bent, making the long front edges crisp and precise. The windows are stainless too, appearing uniform with the counters and range hood and surround.

FLOOR ▼ ▶

Painted the same intense blue as the enamel of the island base, the floor is stenciled with a random pattern of stylized citrus sections.

COLOR

Vibrant color and bright white play together with zest to give this kitchen more than a little retro verve. It's not just the palette of sky blue, turquoise, avocado, and yellow that surprises; it's where the color is placed—countertops, floor, ceiling, and island base, as well as the more expected stove backsplash—and all the shiny materials.

STOVE WALL

Harlequin tiling fills the space between the upper and lower cabinets and the stove and hood—this stove has no integral backsplash so the effect is particularly striking even though the space is not large. Blue interiors showing through the glass of the upper cabinets and the blue counters balance the tiling; the clock is a fittingly whimsical accent.

MEDITATIVE MOOD

With all the essentials but the refrigerator on one wall, and a pared aesthetic that favors clean lines and subdued details, this alcove kitchen is quiet. The repeating horizontals of the hanging shelves, steel backsplash, and cabinetry make no pretense of hiding the low, wide proportions of the room; instead, they give it an honest, unadorned serenity.

ISLAND

The island frame is poured concrete, honed to a soft finish that contrasts with the polished concrete floor. The chopping block with integral prep sink is the room's crowning glory: it's the one "natural" component in the décor, with impressive proportions that allow it to hold its own against the industrial metal and concrete surfaces.

ARCHITECTURAL DETAIL

Classic panels, moldings, and pilasters tie these cabinets to their surroundings, giving this kitchen a traditional look borrowed from a library or living room. Adding to this effect is the stove alcove, which is trimmed like a fireplace, with a mantel supported by decorative brackets, and lined with large brick-shaped green tiles.

FLOOR

The ceramic floor features several sizes of rectangular tiles laid to resemble a terrace; the honey tones and irregular surface offer a warm contrast to the more formal cabinetry.

ACCENTS

Two styles of brass pulls ornamenting the cabinets and the pendant light with ribbed glass shades over the island are fittingly traditional. Simple square wooden stools painted in candy colors break the mold and add some fun.

AMBIENCE

Country charm fills this eat-in kitchen: tints of blue—including the marble countertops, cabinets with simple but classic detail, hints of rusticity in the old bench, trestle table, and terrific faux-beamed ceiling. Checked curtains and the painted stairway in the background add to the homey feeling.

FLOOR

Pale blue squares stained in a checkerboard pattern on the wood-plank floor are the traditional country alternative to a rug or tiles; the diagonal orientation is lively and makes the room seem wider.

PALETTE

Milk, cream, and butter hues permeate this country kitchen. They're gentler and dreamier than crisp white, yet perfectly fresh—a good choice in a room that has old-time charm but works with modern efficiency. The blue lamp shade is a pretty complement and the butcher block countertop adds warmth.

STORAGE

Base cabinets and the island offer lots of concealed storage; plate racks, open shelves, and a few upper cabinets with glass doors provide decorative storage that keeps the ambience light and airy.

NICE EXTRAS

The translucent roll-up shade provides an informal filter for the sunlight. The faucets have simple elegance and an old-fashioned aesthetic. The cabinet to the right of the sink under the window is really a pullout door that holds a wastebasket—scraps can be wiped right into it.

MIX OF OLD AND NEW

The sensitive update of this turn-of-the-last-century beach-house kitchen is fresh but true to the mid-century aesthetic of an earlier "modernization." Notable for their retro character are the large sink, which features an integral backsplash and drain board that tops the cabinet below, and the laminate counters that are faced with a ribbed metal band. The commercial stove couldn't be more contemporary, yet looks right at home.

COLORS

Buttercup walls, a moss ceiling, and natural pine floor give the room a soft background that's pretty and cheerful but feels cozy even under the bright seaside light. The white cabinets and shelves make a clean contrast, feel right for the nostalgic look, and keep the space open.

ACCENTS

Streamlined bar stools, the overhead light fixtures, the schoolroom clock, and colorful crockery all add to the period atmosphere. The clever window counter is inviting yet unobtrusive.

COLOR

Blink again. Here an astonishing citrus yellow streams over the floor and board backsplash, setting pure white cabinets into stark relief. Minimal touches of stainless steel break the spell.

ISLAND

The outside face of the island has storage cabinets at one end but is cut away at the other end to create a small eating counter, which is supported at the open end by a bracket—leaving more of the brilliant floor exposed and making the island less blocky.

ACCENTS

Stainless-steel stools complement the faucet and the backsplash behind the cooktop; the plum and citrus fabric echoes the steel and yellow hues; the glass canisters and vase are interesting for the way they disappear as the color shows through them.

COUNTRY MODERN

Classic in design, with soft colors and cabinets with simple panel doors, this galley kitchen is compactly laid out and opens on one side to living space so that the cook is never isolated. Commercial appliances, marble countertops, and an elegant faucet at the under-mounted sink are contemporary features with timeless appeal.

WINDOW SEAT

Hanging baskets slide into cubbyholes under the cushioned banquette at the end of the work area—they're good-looking and much easier to access than storage under a lift-up seat. The Arts and Crafts–style fabrics used for the tie-up valance and throw pillows have a sophisticated period flavor.

SCALE

This small kitchen has everything one needs to turn out good food with ease and style: commercial-style refrigerator, oven, dishwasher, and cooktop; a microwave concealed in the chamber above the oven; enough cabinetry to hold essential pantry supplies, cookware, and dinnerware; and a big table to supplement the counter area.

TABLE VERSUS ISLAND

In such a small area, a table offers as much work surface as an island and, being leggy rather than closed in, looks much lighter. This one has drawers to supplement the cabinets. Plus, the lower work surface is ideal for rolling out pastry.

NICE EXTRAS

A backsplash of tiny marble tiles reflects the light, and stainless pulls on the dark cabinets complements the appliances.

REPURPOSED ▼ ▶

A vintage ice cream counter found in an architectural salvage shop steals the show in this family-friendly kitchen. Made entirely of marble, with stainless-steel doors, its interior has been retrofitted from freezer to pantry storage. The other cabinets in the room are topped with the same black-and-gold marble and fitted with similar box latches and old-fashioned bin pulls.

MIX OF OLD AND NEW

Classic white subway tile makes an uncomplicated backdrop to both new and old cupboards and industrial-style open stainless shelves, and a rustic wood table flanked by contemporary metal chairs makes informal meals inviting.

CHILD-SAFE ▶

Slots in the back of the counter keep knives out of the reach of small hands.

NICE EXTRA ▼

The wall-mounted faucet over the sink sports a soap dish—handy and charming.

DOMESTIC ELEGANCE ◀ ▲

With an enviable amount of work surface and a place to store everything when not in use, this modern kitchen reminds one of the setup in an old villa: the ample space is inviting and meant to be used, there are no upper cabinets to block the copious daylight, and small appliances and cooking gear are out of sight.

OPEN AND AIRY

Two stories tall, with windows at each level and topped by a skylight, the kitchen enjoys so much natural light that the overhead fixtures are rarely used except at night.

ISLAND WORK SPACE

Two sinks and a commercial stove are along the walls, leaving the ten-foot-long island totally open for prep and serving, with equal access along all sides.

HONED FOR AN AGED LOOK

To make the kitchen feel less modern, the Carrara marble countertops are honed instead of polished, giving them a soft, worn, used look.

NICE EXTRA

A restaurant staple, the heavy-duty, pre-rinse sprayer at one of the sinks takes a first pass at greasy pans before they go into the dishwasher.

Traditional

Let's call it "traditional now"—classic décor with perennial style and a twist of contemporary personality. Moldings and other architectural details can help to set the stage, but the key is a blend of classic furnishings that is neither museum-like nor strongly modernist, with an ambience that's comfortable and reflects the taste of the occupants. This kitchen is a fine example.

• The lofty proportions of the contemporary home are softened by hand-some moldings on all the windows and the subtle texture of subway tile and bead-board. The dark floor grounds the space.

• The overall look is that of an old-fashioned English kitchen. Traditional panel doors and drawers front the lower cabinets; the upper ones are kept light with glass doors and dressed up with brackets and cornice moldings that complement the architecture. Turned posts give a table-like finish to the large island.

• The alcove built to house the range has the feel of a grand fireplace; it masks the exhaust hood and is finished with a mantel-like shelf that is great for display.

• Family and friends are always welcome here—the island and banquette invite everyone to chat, help, or snack while meals are prepped, or to enjoy breakfast or tea.

• Blue and white is a classic color scheme. The yellow wall is a wonderful surprise that warms the room. The rich colors set off the pure white cabinets, tile, and woodwork, absorbing some of the brilliant light without diminishing the sunny ambience, while the white shows off accessories and edibles to advantage.

• Fabrics integrate the colors from one area to another and the jaunty stripes are fun. The Roman shades above the sink are clean and crisp—a softer treatment would be too fussy.

Details that look good and work hard

You probably spend quite a bit of time in your kitchen—working and socializing—so why not incorporate details that make it efficient, great-looking, and a pleasure to use and be in?

A shelf under the exhaust hood keeps accessory equipment handy and looks handsome. ▲

Keep a large wooden cutting board handy to protect your countertops and knives. ◄

If you need a stepladder to reach things stored in upper cabinets, consider one that is also a stool so that a friend can pull it up to your work area for an afternoon chat. ►

Generous open storage at the end of an island makes it easy to stack and access large, heavy cooking equipment. ◄

If you enjoy searching for recipes online, or ordering your groceries electronically, find a dry spot for a small computer. ►

Add a window seat! This one makes it possible to breakfast in a tiny kitchen, masks a radiator, and creates a deep windowsill shelf, too. ▲

CHEFS SPEAK

Celebrity chefs offer these great tips for making your kitchen the best.

"Maximize the use of lower storage space. The higher a space is, the harder it is to work with. The exception to that is slotted storage. I have a cabinet above my wall ovens with ten structured slots for cutting boards and sheet pans, but everything else is down low—mostly in huge drawers. We have a large island as well and had cabinets built along one side that holds all our glasses and plates so that my 5-foot 2-inch wife and 4-foot daughter can reach anything anytime."

ALTON BROWN

"We're redesigning an 1850s farmhouse on Long Island, and I've insisted that the kitchen flow right into the family room, unobstructed, so I can spend time with my guests. Everybody's always in the kitchen anyway—they might as well be comfortable."

TOM COLICCHIO

"Efficiency of flow is what it's all about. From cold station to cutting board to stove to trash to recyclables: all of it has to be organized so that your movements are fluid and you're not backtracking against yourself."

DAN BARBER

"Multiple sinks and work stations are great if you have five people helping you cook, but if it's just you, a small kitchen where everything is within arm's reach is all you need. One great cutting board, one sharp knife, one great pot, and you're set. It's about cooking; it's not about the stuff."

SUZANNE GOIN

"If anything, customize your countertop height. Chopping vegetables, washing up, standing or cooking at a counter, sink, or stove that is the wrong height for you will give you a lot of discomfort, if not an enduringly bad back."

NIGELLA LAWSON

"I could say great lighting or adequate work space. But I think what's more important is to create a room that feels like you—then you'll want to be in it. In my own kitchen, I have various collections that reflect my history and my feelings toward food. I collect vintage bread wrappers and have them framed. Bread has always been such an important part of my life, and these wrappers always make me feel good."

NANCY SILVERTON

"I like natural materials and clean, uninterrupted lines. A sealed concrete floor, tongue-in-groove Shaker cabinetry, teak countertops, and a long teak island look beautiful to me. People have gotten carried away with gadgets, but certain equipment does matter—a great stove can improve cooking, and two dishwashers make entertaining much easier."

BEN FORD

"Rather than honed marble countertops, which stain easily, I often use black or white Formica. I like wood floors—they have a little give to them and are much better to stand on than stone or tile. And I do a kitchen you can eat in whenever possible. That way, all your guests feel like family."

INA GARTEN

BATHROOMS

What qualities are important in your bathroom? A soothing, dreamy ambience? A bright, pristine aura? Sleek modern aesthetics or classic styling? Sophistication? Romance? Charm? Be sure the room includes everything needed to be functional as well as stylish.

Fixtures

Of course, every bathroom needs a toilet, a sink, and a tub or shower, or both. Add a bidet if it appeals. Check a showroom to see different materials options as well as styles; these pieces set the tone for your overall look.

Hardware

Faucets and controls, showerheads, towel rods, cabinet pulls—these are the jewelry in the room, and each piece requires a decision. Know the size requirements for your fixtures before deciding on the fittings.

Cabinets

If you're including a vanity or built-in cupboards, consider style, color, and surface. Custom cabinets will give you the most flexibility for special layout configurations and also style details, but there are myriad excellent stock options, too. If you're doing a master bath, decide if you wish to use a double vanity, two separate ones, or just one.

Surfaces

Choices for stone, ceramic, wood, and synthetic materials abound for floors, countertops, and walls. Paint and wallpaper are options for walls and ceilings as well. Consider water-resistance, color, texture, and pattern in each material.

Window treatments

Privacy is a key concern, so be sure there is a way to make the windows opaque. Shades and blinds are discreet, or go for curtains or draperies if you want something soft.

Lighting

You need general lighting for the room and task lighting at the vanity and in the shower; ambient light from sconces or a chandelier adds atmosphere.

Seating

Totally optional, but a chair, chaise, or bench will make it easy to relax, hold towels or robes, and give a companion a place to perch while you soak.

GLAMOUR ▲ ▶

Dark floors and cabinets, pale aqua walls, a
classic soaking tub, and silk-shaded sconces
give this spacious bathroom an elegance
that's neither too masculine nor too feminine. Elements that catch and bounce the
light make it sparkle: marble, mirrors, a
dressy chandelier, glass drops on the silver-
plated sconces, and cut-glass pulls on the
drawers and shower door.

VANITY

The long double vanity offers generous
his-and-her space, with lots of storage
in the handsome cabinets. Individual
mirrors in silver-toned frames add to the
dressy ambience.

SHOWER

A luxurious, large showerhead, suspended
from the middle of the ceiling, provides a
generous downpour and gives bathers
plenty of room to move.

NICE EXTRAS

A marble mosaic border runs around the
room and also frames the shower window,
and a Plexiglas chair sparkles by the tub.

TIP

*Use mirrors to bounce daylight around
the bathroom. Choose divided frames to
make large mirrors less overwhelming
and more intriguing.*

TAILORED ▲ ▶

Sparkling in the sunlight and formally outfitted with a sleek tub turned sideways (allowing both ends to support a leaning back), a vanity and side tables trimmed with framed-circle motifs, a marble floor and wainscoting, and lots of beveled mirrors, this bath is crisp, clean, dressy, and spacious enough to include a simple chaise for relaxing.

COLOR

Light tones of blue and green provide a restful, watery complement to the bright whites.

DRESSING AREA

A small hallway leading from the bath to the adjacent bedroom is lined with closets and built-in bureaus. Light from both rooms and the overhead fixtures is reflected in the mirrored doors.

DRESSING TABLE

At the bedroom end of the hallway, a dressing table provides space for grooming away from the damp bathroom.

NICE EXTRAS

The hook mounted outside the closet can hold a robe or assembled outfit and the upholstered stools are convenient when putting on shoes.

AMBIENCE

Everything about this bath is capacious, restrained, and elegant in its simplicity, with small tiles creating a shimmering background to the dreamy white tub, dark chair, and fresh green leaves: enter here to be immersed in peaceful solitude and deep warm water.

CHANDELIER

Dripping with crystal, the graceful chandelier adds a romantic touch and sends light dancing over the glazed surfaces.

LAYOUT

Like a private wing, a large alcove shelters the tub in this bathroom, setting aside the best view for a good soak. The vanity, where less time is spent, is around the corner, with a large mirror to catch the daylight.

TUB

The generous tub surround doubles as a counter for spa accessories and a bench— for graceful access to the tub or a companionable chat.

FLOOR

Tiles set with a diagonal lattice link the alcove with the interior and balance the grand moldings that frame it.

PALETTE

Clean and pristine, but not cold all-white; the room is warmed by beige countertops, the tiles that form the lattice, and the lace-pattern wallpaper.

AMBIENCE ▼ ►

Bold alternating bands of limestone and marble line this gentleman's bath, making it modern yet not clinical, luxurious yet not glitzy, and masculine without being dark. They're graphic, too, which suits the modern aesthetic of the accoutrements.

VANITY

A rosewood console converted to house a sink and topped with limestone, the vanity looks streamlined and poised on slender legs. It lends the bath a furnished appearance very different from that of built-in cabinets; the wall-mounted controls accentuate that effect.

SHOWER

A double casement window and stone garden bench give a poetic accent to the walk-in
shower, which is lavishly fitted at one end
with various showerheads. The enclosure is
large enough to be open at the opposite
end—with a limestone-topped curb to catch
the water—bringing the fresh air from the
window into the room.

NICE EXTRAS

The niche in the shower wall for shampoo,
and the hook at the open end, where a towel
stays dry, are both thoughtful elements here.

AMBIENCE

Soft, very full white curtains trimmed with tassel fringe lend a feminine touch to this combination dressing and bathroom, where blue walls make a pretty background to classic white woodwork.

ACCOUTREMENTS

Pretty is the word—the bright brass hardware, needlework pictures of bygone times, a chair with a gathered skirt, blue-and-white waste bin, footed bowl, and other vanity accessories are sprightly and fresh.

LAYOUT

The tub nicely fills the space created by a closet that projects into the room; the vanity takes advantage of a bay window.

SIMPLICITY

A creamy palette, subtle play of angles and curves, and spare, modern aesthetic fill this bathroom with soothing harmony.

TEXTURE

Painted paneling creates a simple, angular background for the gracious rounded contours of the tub and vanity basin. The tufted, damask-pattern rug puts a creamy screen over the dark wood floor.

ACCENTS

A simple metal table holds accessories next to the tub and a surprising old metal chest on a matching stand holds reading material across the room—their dark patina fitting gently into the creamy space.

TIP

Indulge in a towel warmer. Warm towels are seductive, of course, but those heated bars will also dry your towel after you've used it— great in humid climates or chilly bathrooms.

PROPORTION

The large mirror over the vanity amplifies the size of this bathroom, where blue tile wainscoting carries the eye around the perimeter and frameless glass transparently encloses the shower.

PATTERNED FLOOR

A large tiled grid brings the wall color onto the floor; the white ground keeps the space feeling light and open.

STORAGE

The tailored vanity provides plenty of storage for necessities, with a white countertop that echoes the floor.

AMENITIES

The shower is fitted with two showerheads—a large one overhead and a smaller handheld unit—as well as corner baskets for toiletries.

AMBIENCE

Step into this room and you'll feel submerged in a lovely blue pool—it's just tile, but it's a total environment. The irregular white, aqua, and blue pattern on the floor is like dappled sunlight filtering through the deeps above.

AMENITIES

A small, slatted bench is affixed to the shower wall and the simple recess is fitted with one shelf.

BASINS

Individual counter-mounted basins adroitly define his-and-her territory at this shared vanity. Their handsome blocky profile has a lot of character, looks snowy and clean against the blue tiles, and provides space for toiletries.

STORAGE

Open cubbyholes fitted with wicker bins add a soft, light accent to the vanity—plus the pullout bins are easier to access than the back of a shelf.

MOTIF

The square—present in mirror, porcelain, tile, and wicker—gives satisfying structure to the vanity, which is composed entirely of right angles.

GRAPHIC

Stark bands of dark walnut, white marble, and blue tile combine handsomely in this bath, where the vanity features open towel cubbies, a taller center cabinet, and two oval mirrors mounted in walnut frames. Round chrome pulls punctuate the cabinet face.

NICE EXTRA

The center cabinet is topped by a piece of mirror, which reflects the view from the window above it as well as the blue ceiling tiles.

BUILT-INS

A built-in vanity, tub, and open storage answer the challenge of this very small bathroom; they're neat, precise, and charmingly integrated with the beadboard walls and ceiling and the marble floor.

TUB

The tub platform is just large enough to hold candles or toiletries; it's supplemented by a basket for soaps and a small table for things that must stay perfectly dry.

NICE EXTRA

Framed prints add a handsome finish, drawing the eye in and breaking up the expanse above the tub.

ROOM WITH A VIEW

This raised tub allows bathers a spectacular view across the adjacent bedroom to the ocean beyond. A sliding shoji screen provides optional privacy.

AMENITY

The small television in the recess above the tub is on an adjustable mount for optimum viewing.

ONE-PIECE DESIGN

The integrated tub, vanity, and step fit the small space efficiently—a clever but uncomplicated arrangement of horizontal and vertical planes. The moss, taupe, and rich brown palette lays a soft tone over the crisp design while defining each component.

AMBIENCE ►

Reverse-painted glass tiles line the walls of
this walk-in shower; the technique imparts a
sense of depth and luminosity to the color,
creating a deeply aquatic effect—refreshing
and magical.

EASE

A white bench floats against the rear wall; it
stays dry unless the hand-held shower is
taken down from its perch on the wall. A
grab bar offers discreet, reassuring security—
these are required by most building codes
and nice to include so handsomely.

MODERN LUXURY

Custom made for this master bath in a
glass high-rise, the tub is cast concrete, with
the rim polished to a glorious sheen. It's in a
mirror-lined alcove that reflects the opposite
shower and skyline.

COLOR

Doors and trim in this room are painted a
dark charcoal green—rich, neutral, quiet,
and striking against the aqua glass tiles and
white concrete.

MASS APPEAL

Blitzed floor to ceiling with polished white marble bricks laid with straight, rather than staggered, joints, this tiny bathroom gives a feeling of total indulgence in modern luxury.

SINK

The asymmetrical pedestal sink has an integral counter cantilevered to one side of the square base, offering maximum surface and looking sharp and modern. It's topped with a minimalist faucet and a towel bar drops below it.

SCALE

Though the room is small, the space is interesting, with a projecting wall backing the sink and holding an unusually tall medicine cabinet with a frameless mirror.

CURVES AND ANGLES

A curved wall faced with vertical boards sets the stage in this modern bath, where sinuous lines shape the top and base of the double vanity and the tub snugs the wall below the window.

AMENITY

The small TV keeps bathers prepped with the day's news or offers a video indulgence to accompany a soothing soak.

MIX OF MATERIALS

Black and white granite, polished on the countertop, honed on the floor, and stainless steel, hammered to a mellow tone to form the tub and smooth and shiny on the vanity, mirror frame, stool, and candle bracket, are an unexpected complement to the painted wood wall.

ARCHITECTURAL DETAIL

Lavish use of mirrors bounces lots of light into this long, narrow bathroom in an effect that's far from sterile. White moldings divide the walls above the vanity into elegant framed sections, which repeat intriguingly on the intersecting walls and mirrored doors.

VANITY

The framed motif is repeated on the double vanity cabinet, which steps out ever so slightly in front of each sink.

FLOOR

Rosy beige marble continues the reflections, adding a warm tint to the light in the mirrors.

COLOR

The rust-colored marble vanity top brings a warm, sunrise contrast to the white board walls in this summerhouse bath; a few wrought-iron accessories punctuate the décor while chrome pieces shine subtly against the white.

AMENITIES

Two adjustable mirrors on stands, each with different magnification, supplement the large one on the wall above the vanity. The chrome-and-glass medicine cabinet is fun— it's a bit industrial, doesn't look bulky, and complements the small étagère below it.

AMBIENCE

Tropical luxury permeates this tub niche, where majestic rustic wood columns frame the entry and a bank of windows wraps the end and opens to lush Hawaiian vegetation. The generous platform around the tub can double as a banquette.

COLOR

Brown travertine marble supplies a sophisticated finish to the spa-like bath, echoing the warm hues of the natural wood used throughout this home and appearing at first glance to be another indigenous material.

AMBIENCE

Set in the whitewashed rustic charm of an old French farmhouse, pure simplicity is the essence of this bathing alcove. Large, footed white tub; high, beamed white ceiling; white walls; a big mirror; white mat on the worn wide floorboards; some towels waiting on a nearby chair; virtually no accessories—here is cleanliness at the ready.

COLOR

A wood floor and a few framed prints in the same hue warm the white room, enhancing the old fashioned simplicity of the setting.

CUPBOARD

A weathered cupboard stands in for a linen closet and frames the left side of the alcove, adding balance to the returning wood wall on the right.

TRADITIONAL NOW

A brick-lined alcove trimmed with cherry-wood molding frames this inviting deep soaking tub with a touch of romance while the floor-mounted bath filler is modern and tailored. On the opposite wall, basins counter-mounted on a marble-topped table give a classic but contemporary twist to the look.

FLOOR

Big square ceramic tiles mimic stone and echo the rustic texture of the brick. A plush carpet warms their surface.

AMENITIES

Lights recessed within the alcove cast a warm glow on the framed prints over the tub, and a chrome basket slides where needed to keep sponges and soaps handy. The small table stands in for a towel bar and holds flowers, a book, or whatever needs to stay dry.

CLASSIC STYLE

Soft colors and attention to detail make this small space, which is in full view of the adjacent bedroom, appealing from without and a pleasure to be in. Paneled wainscoting makes a pretty frame for the room and a marble floor laid in a delicate mosaic pattern adds a nuanced glow; it is highlighted by the random tonal variations of the stone and set within a block border.

CHALLENGING LAYOUT

The pair of windows off-center precluded a double vanity with mirrors for two on the end wall. Instead, the leggy console sinks suit the classic aesthetic, sit lightly in the space, and allow back-to-back mates a view of one another in their facing mirrors.

NICE EXTRAS

The narrow shelf capping the wainscoting is just deep enough for toiletries, the whisper-fine linen curtains filter the sunlight, and the framed nude balances the windows and adds a little wit.

NAUTICAL LOOK

Wave-like borders, painted around the mirror and sewn to the shower curtain, give this bare-bones bath a splash of style. The natural sisal rug adds a sand-colored accent to the seaside scheme.

CONSOLE SINK

A tailored skirt trimmed with blue stripes makes a jaunty cover for under-sink storage—an easy, inexpensive alternative to a vanity cabinet.

SMALL AS CAN BE

Perfectly proportioned old-fashioned fixtures fit snugly in this tiny room, where
everything white looks pure and charming.

TUB SHOWER

White curtains whispering around the tub
enclose the shower; they're hung on an overhead ring that's suspended from the ceiling
at one end, from the wall at the other.

AMENITIES

The elaborately carved open box mounted
over the pedestal sink frames a mirror;
painted white, it's unexpected and appealing
and sits lightly above the diminutive
glass shelf.

COLOR ◄ ▼

A wake-up palette of red and white says a cheerful "good-morning" in this small bath.

SCALE

Perfectly proportioned, the traditionally detailed fixtures are charming yet don't crowd the room. Being leggy, the console sink and claw-foot tub keep the room looking open, while the tiled wainscoting protects against splashes and the stylized pastoral print wallpaper adds color without closing in on the space.

AMENITIES

The sink has an integral backsplash and is fitted with towel bars, and the small glass shelf has a little railing. The tub is fitted with a handheld shower and a toiletries basket with a book rack; there's an accordion shaving mirror over the tub, as well as a small metal-and-glass shelf unit—all sitting lightly in the space while making it a pleasure to use.

AMBIENCE

This engaging, whimsically romantic little bathroom is full of mirrored sparkle, trimmed with fanciful accessories, and glowing with old-rose and amber hues.

COMPOSITION

The juxtaposition of dark and light is very effective here—mirrored cabinets nearly disappearing in the reflected opposite tiles, the wainscoting stepping up behind the white pedestal sink and down to lengthen the windows, the raised shades taking the color up to the top of the windows, and the sconce shades carrying the hues above the mirror.

NEW TRADITIONAL

Here, a modern, frameless glass shower mixes with classic cabinets with paneled doors, complementary paneled shutters in the windows, beadboard on the walls and raised ceiling, gleaming cherrywood floors, and an old-fashioned claw-foot tub for a look of timeless elegance.

LAYOUT

The transparent shower enclosure maximizes the space in this long, narrow room, where windows on two walls limit layout options. The shower stands, nearly invisible, between the two vanities and opposite the footed tub.

Luxurious

To conjure a look of glamour and elegance, imagine you live in a five-star hotel suite, where luxury is easy and refined, not ostentatious. Think a mix of velvety and glossy surfaces, satin finishes and metallics—the finest materials used with gracious sensitivity. This bathroom is a perfect example.

• The room is made special from the outset by its oval shape; note the restrained details that pamper and relax—like the incredibly comfortable chairs, which are upholstered in the softest terrycloth and make this much more than a place to wash up.

• The palette of soft white, antique gold, and silver pairs with contrasting gleaming and matte surfaces that glow softly or absorb the light to give the space a spa-like aura.

• Seemingly simple, the floor is a tour de force, with a ring of honey onyx framing triangles of white marble that converge on an onyx medallion.

• Silver leaf on the ceiling tops the room with magical elegance and reflects the play of water in the tub. A chandelier with lovely proportions adds a sparkling grace note.

• It's a small touch, but the double door at the end hints at ceremony, and when fully open, lies unobtrusively against the entry walls.

• The vanities (there are two; only one is seen here) are glamorous mirrored chests, converted to hold the basins. The reflective fronts and the mirrored walls above them make each touch of luxury more so, repeating every surface, color, and subtle detail.

Home Spa

You're busy so much of the time, so why not make your bathroom a place for pampering, relaxation, and dreaming? The room need not be huge, just thoughtfully outfitted and styled with a soothing aesthetic. Here's an example.

A palette of white, wheat, terra-cotta, and walnut looks clean but not at all clinical and sets a gentle, sophisticated tone. Watery or creamy colors might seem dreamier to you— look through this chapter for more inspiration. Lots of natural light is refreshing, and mirrors make the most of it.

Add fresh flowers, candles, lights on dimmers, a sound system, and the best plush towels. Then walk in and linger. ▲

There's nothing as relaxing as a good soak, so include a deep tub with ends angled for leaning back. Elegant hardware makes you feel like royalty—indulge in a design that makes you smile every time you enter the room. A handheld shower-head makes rinsing a breeze. ▲

A desk-height counter with a magnifying mirror allows you to sit for makeup, a manicure, or even letter writing; it needn't be built in—use a dressing table if you prefer and there's room. ▼

When it's time to pick up the pace, walk into a wonderful shower enclosure. The more showerheads or sprays, the more invigorating the experience. This one, tiled in a tessellated pattern and closed with pretty curtains, has a romantic elegance to match the room; a frameless glass enclosure would be a sleek, modern alternative. ▼

A gorgeous floor makes the room special; this one is marble, with a border shaped to echo the curved base of the walk-in shower. Have cushy mats on hand for wet feet or cold mornings. ▲

DESIGNERS SPEAK

Bathrooms are meant to pamper. Here some people in the know share the whims they indulge.

"A scale that tops out at 107, a mirror that makes me look tall and thin, and a tub that sleeps fourteen with a window that over-looks a garden."

JOAN RIVERS *Comedienne*

"A really comfortable chair for someone to sit on and talk to me while I'm in the bath. And a handy ledge or a little nearby table that's big enough to hold a glass of Champagne."

KATHRYN M. IRELAND *Interior Designer*

"I like simple baths, but I do like to wear those nice gloves you can scrub your skin smooth with, and I always keep Fels Naptha soap because we have a lot of poison ivy around and it's good for poison ivy."

CHIPPY IRVINE *Writer*

"Over-the-top towels made from 650 grams per square inch of the finest Cairo Egyptian cotton. Of course, they need to be bound in a combed cotton contrast and embellished with a custom-designed monogram— all to coordinate with the bathroom's décor." ELLIE CULLMAN *Interior Designer*

"I like to take a bouquet of flowers, put it in a mirrored corner of the bathroom, open the door—I actually reversed the way my door swings so this would work—and enjoy the view of the bath from my bed."

ALEXANDRA STODDARD
Author and Interior Designer

"My ultimate bath indulgence begins with stepping into my bamboo-enclosed out-door shower that overlooks my garden, standing under the sunflower-size deluge showerhead with plenty of hot water while I lather up with my favorite big bar of Santa Maria Novella pomegranate soap."
MISH TWORKOWSKI
Jewelry Designer

"Artwork: certainly unexpected, but given how much time one spends in the bathroom, it's always appreciated."

ALEXA HAMPTON
Interior Designer

BEDROOMS

What sort of ambience would you like your bedroom to have? Dreamy, serene, luxurious, pristine, relaxed, spare, intimate, cozy, or flamboyant? Whatever your preference, you'll want it to be a private sanctuary conducive to repose, relaxation, and happiness.

A good bed

The style of the bed frame will set the tone of your room. Consider whether hangings and a canopy are part of your dream, if a platform design is appealing, or what sort of posts, headboard, and footboard, if any, you prefer. Consider the height from floor to top of mattress for aesthetics and also ease of use.

Tables

Something at the bedside is essential for holding books, eyeglasses, and a lamp: a nightstand, candlestand, and small chest are all options; choose something that looks balanced in the available space. If there is room, a desk or dressing table may be desirable as well.

Comfortable seating

If the room is large enough for a sitting area, include as much upholstered seating as fits. If not, provide one comfy chair or a chaise so that you can read, and a side chair—everyone needs to sit while putting on shoes.

Lighting

Ambient light sets the mood, so choose lamps, sconces, perhaps a chandelier. Make sure there's good reading light by the bed (articulated wall fixtures give the most flexibility) and next to upholstered seating or at a desk.

Storage

Depending on how much closet space there is and your style preferences, you may need an armoire, dressers for folded clothes, or a blanket chest. Make provision for a television if you wish.

Window treatments

Choose whatever type is appropriate for your decorating style, but be sure there's a way to provide privacy and also to filter or block the sun if that is important to you.

Floor covering

The choice of a large carpet or rug, or several small ones strategically placed is personal and depends on the overall look you favor. Whichever you prefer, your bare feet will be happiest if there is something to cover a cold floor.

Linens

The bedclothes are part of the décor, so don't treat them as an afterthought. They may be coordinated with the window treatments, if you like, or simply complement the overall aesthetic.

AMBIENCE

Deep, unpatterned hues, tall proportions, luxe linens, curtains that match the walls, and a few intriguing accessories make this room a cocoon for tranquil repose. The volume of the dark colors—sapphire and ocean blue, and copper—invites you to just sink down and sleep.

HEADBOARD

Panels of plain, copper-toned wood form a soaring, simple, architectural backdrop at the head of the bed.

SPARE AESTHETIC

Ocean light, ceilings fifteen feet high, and a scrupulously detailed yet unaccessorized aesthetic combine with impressive simplicity in this beach-house bedroom. The platform bed and horizontal lines on the upholstered screen and dark, lower portion of the back wall ground the space while the sheer curtain that divides the sleeping area from the bath soars toward the sky.

MIX OF MATERIALS

With a palette limited to sand, ocean, and white, and the only pattern the graphic divisions on the screen and back wall, the texture of each of the various materials comes into focus: polished concrete floor, wood platform, hide rug, bed linens, folds in the curtain, and metal brads delineating the grid on the screen.

BED

The platform bed is as close to lying on the beach as one might wish indoors. Lamps suspended from the ceiling with black cord share the spare aesthetic and accentuate the dramatic proportions.

NICHE ▼ ►

A bed set in a recess feels secure and intimate. Here, grandly proportioned moldings frame a newly constructed niche with a modern interpretation of old-world detail.

COLOR

White trim outlines areas of color—brilliant pomegranate lining the niche paired with sophisticated pastels. The upholstery on the bed is the same pomegranate with a moiré pattern that gives a cue to the pink used elsewhere.

BEDSIDE TABLES

Paired by wood tone and scale rather than form, a small desk and pedestal table flank the bed.

CARPET

Naive, Japanese-style flowers tossed with confidence on a surprising, oversize glen plaid background give a lively finish to the room, happily supporting the very personal assortment of contemporary and traditional furnishings.

CASUAL CHIC

A big potted palm, a cheerful assortment of furniture, and lots of white to reflect the sunlight set a summery tone here. With turned posts, a cane headboard, and fresh white linens, the bed has a lot of character; the cane bench complements it, the slipcovered club chair is ready for relaxing.

ASIAN ACCENTS

Cherry-colored with gold accents, depicting fanciful flying birds, the Chinese rug covers the floor exuberantly. The ceramic garden stool has graceful piercings, adds another interesting form, and connects indoors to out; plus, the color is great against the buttery slipcover.

BRICK WALL

Painted white, the brick wall adds an interesting textured background—left natural, it would dominate the space.

KIMONO

If you are a lover of fine textiles, let one take the place of a headboard—it will do just as much to set the style of your room and be unique as well. This graceful kimono has beautiful color and a delicate pattern.

BEDDING

Pure white and bright orange linens, sans pattern, pick up and amplify the colors of the kimono; the white pillows keep the kimono silhouetted and discrete.

AMBIENCE

Comfortable and cheerful—flowers and the hot-water-bottle cozy are beckoning.

NEW ROMANTIC

Lovely hand-painted wallpaper and an antique mantel imbue this bedroom with old-world elegance. Mirrors, on the divided light doors and over the fireplace, bring in and reflect light. The plush carpet, velvet headboard, and generous array of pillows add a simple, sensuous invitation to relax.

COLOR

Antique, tea-stain gold, powder blue, ivory, white, and hints of smoke combine in a palette of quiet, soothing hues. The pure white linens look crisp and fresh; everything else has an air of gentle, comfortable age.

PATTERN

The striped bed skirt pays a perfect compliment to the wallpaper; the only other pattern is the stripe accents on the headboard, linens, and lampshades.

AMBIENCE

This bedroom—in a new house with décor that's lightly traditional with modern accents—has all the attributes of the perfect guest room: a comfortable bed, nightstand, clock, chair, and reading lamp. The vase of flowers is a nice touch with which to welcome overnight visitors. The color scheme—note the cluster of green on the nightstand and the green trim on the chair—and botanical-print wallpaper contribute to the room's old-fashioned mood.

BED

The antique barley-twist bed infuses the cozy room with cottage style. With its generous headboard and beautiful white linens with pink accents, the bed invites guests to settle in for a good night's sleep.

EASY LUXURY

Smoky mirrors lining the niche around this bed head cast the room and the reflected décor in sophisticated light. The bed, handsomely dressed in tones of wheat and ivory, has no visible frame but wears a pleated velvet skirt ornamented with matching buttons, a generous comforter, and elegantly embroidered pillows.

SIDE TABLES

Three shelves and a drawer take care of bedside wants most attractively.

SIMPLE COMFORT

A stylish easy chair, a platform bed wrapped in taupe and white and topped with big plump pillows, and a simply striped shag rug provide the essentials here: a place to sit, a place to sleep, and something nice to greet bare feet. Add the lamps and side tables and one important piece of art, color it all in natural sandy hues, and peace ensues.

MIX OF MATERIALS

A vaulted ceiling with exposed beams, natural cedar walls, and a stone floor lead all eyes to the glass doors at the end of this room.

BUILT-INS

Cupboards and closets, built discreetly into the wall across from the bed, harmonize with the opposite plank wall and keep possessions out of sight.

SYMMETRY

Placing a bed directly in front of windows is uncommon, but here, where the peaked ceiling and paired gable windows prescribe the focus, it's a natural, keeping the layout centered and equally divided. On each side, a country candlestand, simple lamp, and pair of framed botanicals complete the symmetry; the single throw pillow and boxy trunk balance the peak above.

BED

The delicate wrought-iron bed frame has a spare, country elegance, looks graphic against the window, carries the eye up, and adds no weight. Plain bed linens with just a touch of color keep the frame silhouetted in the space.

AMBIENCE

The exposed, old post-and-beam structure and large wood mantel provide this room with a backdrop of country history that's enhanced by traditional scalloped valances over long curtains. The old quilt and pretty print fabrics in a simple green-and-white color scheme make it fresh and inviting.

BED-SITTER

Comfy club chairs, an upholstered bench at the foot of the bed, and two armchairs make it clear that this room is enjoyed during waking hours, with the fireplace lighted and savored.

TAILORED

Here, a plain, upholstered panel spans the lower portion of the wall behind the bed, anchoring the adjustable lamps and providing a backdrop to the mirror-topped side tables as well as the bed. The curvy quilting on the bolster and bedspread introduces a bit of softness, contrasting the crisp Roman shades on the window and large-scale gingham covering the pillows.

PALETTE

Pale green walls, gold, ivory, and cinnamon distinguish this neutral scheme.

TIP

A reading light with a dimmer and good narrow focus, on an articulated arm, is an essential bedside amenity.

MODERN ROMANCE

An occasional blush of pink adds a feminine softness to this tailored room, which is large and dressed with restraint. The dark throw at the foot of the bed is mink—a sensuous touch.

SCALE

A tray ceiling increases the spacious feeling, all the furnishings are simply detailed, with monochrome, sometimes textured, surfaces, and scaled to balance it. The tall, quilted, upholstered headboard was designed to ground the room, replicating the effect of a mantelpiece in a room with a fireplace.

SITTING AREA

With so much room, the sitting area feels separate from the sleeping quarters. Two club chairs share a big round ottoman and the view through the nearby window.

BED

A wraparound headboard embraces this bed and holds it securely in a wider window alcove. The freestanding board has a stylized top contour and is outlined with metal studs; the arms are just deep enough to enclose the bedside tables. The companion footboard is simpler, masks the bedding from the nearby sitting area, and forms a back for the bench that fronts it.

COLOR

The ivory bed, carpet, and walls are a foil for the brilliant colors that accent the room. Patterned silks add an exotic touch.

WINDOW TREATMENT

A taupe border on the top, bottom, and outside edges of the translucent jade-color draperies creates a frame for the bed. A wide Roman shade provides privacy when needed.

BALANCE

This bed is centered between two side tables, but not centered in the overall space. The higher, smaller table on the left balances the wider, shorter table on the right, and the headboard keeps an even weight between them—a simple device and good reminder that asymmetry can be interesting.

COLOR

A deft eye chose the apple green that pops behind the blackish-brown headboard, indigo and bright blue, turquoise, silver-gray, and hints of purple. The whites keep the other colors separate and clean.

TUCKED AWAY

This alcove barely accommodates a bed and two side tables, but it's pretty as can be and full of the promise of sweet dreams.

OLD AND NEW

Aged surfaces on the bed, bench, and tables, a vintage rag rug, and charming old plates on the wall mix with fresh linens, painted white floor, and softly gathered lampshades in classic country cottage style.

COLOR

Sky blue against white—the beloved, country-fresh combination—wafts like fresh breezes over this small room, where lace curtains fill the windows, the floor is painted, and the furnishings are eclectic. With not even a hint of another color, the effect is particularly striking.

BEDS

High, decorative footboards give the twin beds an old-world, storybook charm.

ROOM WITH A VIEW

The framework securing the glass wall is all that separates this bedroom from the view opening out beyond and below it; the modern, all-white décor offers no distraction to the vista and the spaces seem to merge in the hot white light that floods the room.

NICHE

The lighted recess above the bed adds dimension to the interior and frames a different view, displaying small sculptures.

WHITE EDGES

Nearly everything in the room is upholstered or wrapped in white; there are very few contrasting elements to interrupt the illusion of continuous space—just the chrome lamps and chair frame, the base of the bench, and the wood side table. Furnishings with varied textures—suede headboard, polished linens, leather bench, and joined-squares rug—ground the space.

COUNTRY MODERN

Board walls painted white, with matching moldings, a bed with the headboard and box spring slipcovered in natural linen, a matching linen spread over white sheets, and a pickled frame on the contemporary graphic—this bedroom is country fresh, stylishly uncomplicated, and comfortable.

ACCESSORIES

The metal frame side tables feature thick board tops, highly polished but with their edges rough-cut. The metal lamps that top them are intriguing, with scaffold-like structure.

NICE EXTRA

The windows are fitted with shades that unroll from the sill—they can be raised to cover the lower portion of the sash for privacy, while leaving the top open to the moonlight or morning sun.

TIP

An upholstered headboard is not purely aesthetic: it gives you a place to recline in bed and read comfortably.

WOOD

The exposed indigenous-wood structure plays a striking role in this Hawaiian home; it's fitting that the bed be natural wood and share the proportions of the trusses above. The frame is made of recycled teakwood and designed with the simple lines typical of colonial Hawaiian furniture.

TEXTILES

Warm, mellow earth tones in ethnic patterns dress the bed elegantly and without pretension. Semi-sheer hanging panels soften the architectural effect of the massive bed frame and add a sense of intimacy. The pillows were custom-embroidered using patterns taken from antique Indonesian baskets.

MIX OF CULTURES

Color unifies textiles of unrelated origin and sensibility to give this bedroom distinctive beauty. On the bed is a coverlet made from vintage Tibetan fabric; on the wall an embroidered eighteenth-century English tapestry.

LESS IS ENOUGH

A few sculptural accessories—some ceramic vessels, the lamp, and the throw pillow—a clock, and a notepad are enough to make the room comfortable; the embroidered backdrop is too extraordinary for competition.

SUMMER COTTAGE
Small proportions, ceiling open to the peak over exposed beams, funny little square windows in the gable wall, a painted board floor, flea-market furnishings, and a background dotted with small sprays of roses make this a hideaway with storybook charm.

BED
Sweet against the roses, the wrought-iron bed is appealingly old-fashioned and sits delicately in the small room. Pure white bedding is simple and feminine.

NICE EXTRAS
Silver and crystal lamps dress up the painted cottage furniture; the vintage white-framed mirror over the bed adds another window.

COLOR

Intense splashes of two primary colors and accents of the third bring the furnishings of this Swedish-style bedroom into bright focus against the white walls and natural carpet. With a high headboard and somewhat lower footboard, the yellow bed makes a cheery home for the red-and-white linens; the red pleated shade on the blue lamp carries the color scheme onto the yellow side table.

PATTERN

Bedclothes, being diverse and layered by nature, offer an easy way to mix patterns. Here, a charming mix of figured and solid linens makes a lively composition.

MIX OF STYLES

Old and new join forces to give this bedroom fresh country style. The bed has bold
turnings with oversize acorn finials and a
headboard with a traditional silhouette,
surprisingly upholstered and outlined with
metal studs. The bench and dressing table
have history; the chairs, lamps, and window
shades are contemporary.

COLOR

Soft blues contrast gently with white, creating a restful ambience—fresh, and pleasantly
quieter than a mix of white with crisp, bright
blues. The ceiling is covered with a blue-
and-white striée wallpaper that emulates
wood beadboard paneling.

NICE EXTRA

The round mirror over the bed fits perfectly,
has an interesting but simple frame, and
picks up the curved shapes introduced by
the headboard, lamp, and side chair.

MIX OF STYLES

In this inviting and comfortable bedroom, neoclassical and contemporary furnishings mix gracefully, united in red and cream. Striped fabric imparts a cheerful formality to the walls and silhouettes the solid-color furnishings; bands cut from it add a calmer accent to the curtains and bed linens. Braided straw matting adds texture and has a timeless quality.

NICE EXTRA

The large clock suspended inside the bed canopy adds an intriguing punctuation mark.

BED

Sheltered by an architectural canopy and embraced by identical high ends, the bed is turned sideways against the wall to greet the room. It's dressed simply, in natural linen with red striped borders, and upholstered in red on the outside.

SYMMETRY

Opposite the window, a chest flanked by a pair of armchairs and topped by symmetrically arranged accessories looks pleasingly composed. The mirror frame is covered in paisley, which gives it an antique look that suits the other furnishings.

BEDCLOTHES ▲ ►

Embroidered sheer curtains tied casually to
the frame enclose the bed head, implying
privacy; with the ivory quilt, scalloped
shams and duvet, and sheer skirt, they dress
the bed with relaxed elegance.

NEW ROMANTIC

A peaked ceiling, exposed beams, delicate
chandelier, four-poster bed, skirted table,
personal mementos, and lots of white hues,
cast a dreamy spell over this large room.

TIP

*Soft layers are romantic: add more pillows
and throws if that's the look you're after.*

ROUND TABLE

Covered to the floor with a quilted cloth, the round table is pretty and understated.

RECESS

A recess opposite the bed withdraws the media cabinet from the traffic area and lightens its impact on the delicate décor.

BAY WINDOW

By nature an inviting place to linger, this bay is hung with simple curtains and blessed with an elegant chair and matching ottoman in the style known as *duchesse brisée*; the black-and-white toile upholstery is fun and fittingly French.

AMBIENCE

Creamy walls, scalloped borders on the formal draperies and bed hangings, and bed linens, settee, and carpet all in plain ivory make this apartment bedroom a tranquil retreat from the city without. The room is spacious, made more so with moldings painted to match the walls and furnishings that are low.

SITTING AREA

The graceful settee in the corner sits in shadow, away from the urban noise and neighborhood windows. Short apothecary floor lamps shed warm, intimate light and keep the focus low.

AMBIENCE

Traditional furnishings and typical fabrics dress this French farmhouse bedroom with comfortable country gentility. White paint brightens the rustic beamed ceiling, the floorboards wear the patina of age, and an armoire attractively substitutes for a nonexistent closet.

BED

A wall canopy and hangings shelter the bed, making it cozy without closing it in. The headboard is upholstered to match the hangings and bed skirt; assorted prints make up the rest of the dressing.

GRACIOUS ▲ ►

This corner bedroom is blessed with natural light on two sides and open to an adjacent sitting room on a third. The rooms share a restrained traditional décor, soft colors with little contrast, a single carpet, and damask upholstery. En suite, they provide private sanctuary to be enjoyed at any hour.

UPHOLSTERED FURNITURE

To create the soothing ambience, there is very little natural wood in this décor; almost everything is either painted a soft color or covered with fabric. The upholstered sleigh bed is generously padded and tufted and the same color as the wall. It's soft, rounded, and sculptural, as are the chairs and sofa in the sitting room.

BEDCLOTHES

A flat, cream-colored coverlet with scalloped
edges and layers of pillows in matching
shams lie lightly on the bed, a simple complement to the more complex contours of
the upholstered form. Discreet monograms
add a sophisticated finish to the shams.

SITTING AREA

With a sofa and two easy chairs gathered
before the fireplace, the sitting room is sized
to welcome family and special friends for
coffee and private conversation. Like the
adjacent bedroom, it's dressy but unpreten-
tious and comfortable, with lots of light.

DETAILS

The wall lamps in the two areas complement
each other but are not the same, each being
suited to its individual space and task.

BED

Dominating this room, the bed frame features an exceptionally tall, upholstered headboard with step-down returns that enclose the mattress, echoed by a lower foot-board with the same design. Sand-colored upholstery and lavender linens contrast the frame and heighten its graphic quality.

WINDOW TREATMENT

For privacy, the end wall may be completely covered by the full-height curtain, which rides on a track mounted on the ceiling and is pieced with a deep band of lavender at the bottom, repeating the horizontal of the bedclothes.

NICE EXTRAS

The metal étagères echo the graphics of the bed. Copper lamps are cleverly suspended from the ceiling.

HEADBOARD
Extending completely across the wall behind this bed, a quilted linen panel is both headboard and very modern wainscoting.

CABINET
Affixed to the headboard, with the illusion that it floats, a storage unit takes the place of a nightstand on each side of the bed.

PALETTE
Warm whites, natural linen, lavender-gray, and toast hues create a nuanced setting for the contemporary photographs the owners collect.

POINT OF VIEW ◄ ▲
Here a curtained bed unexpectedly pulled away from the walls frames an enticing view of the fireplace and creates a room within a room.

PATTERN
Watery blue-on-white fabric on the bed and windows and chalky white-on-blue wallpaper lend romance to the room. Reversed backgrounds separate the two while creating an overall harmony.

NIGHTSTANDS
The blue ottoman takes the place of a nightstand, keeping the prospect from the doorway soft and romantic. On the far side of the bed, a writing desk complements the fireside sitting area.

WINDOW TREATMENT
Draperies installed over the crown molding, drawn back high above the sill, and puddling gently on the floor, add a pretty vertical and seem to raise the ceiling. Relaxed Roman shades provide privacy.

LIGHTING
Ambient light keeps a bedroom tranquil, and here hanging lanterns fill each corner with glowing candlelight. A few lamps provide reading light.

DETAILS
Framed wallpaper panels—one on each side of the door—become art with period flavor. A neoclassical étagère provides an ornate setting for small decorative objects. Tassels—on cabinets and upholstery, add a dressy finishing touch.

Scandinavian

Washes of pale, pretty color, checks and stripes, delicate carved and painted furniture, and overall simplicity are the hallmarks of traditional Swedish style, which is often called "Gustavian" after the eighteenth-century monarch. Swedish furniture of that period was very influenced by French design and the resulting look is the charming mix of formal and country elements seen in this bedroom.

- Walls painted aged cream above a chair rail and pale grayed green below and wide pine floorboards rubbed with liming paste wrap the room in soft color. The cream-color furniture sits lightly in the space, adding subtle detail.

- This carved and upholstered bed is terrific—it's French, and it fits right in with the Swedish pieces.

- Graphic and vibrant, the raspberry checks and pink stripes are fun against the soothing background colors. We love the way the subtler print on the duvet and pillows picks up the entire palette.

- With ample space on both sides of the bed, the small chests are a good alternative to nightstands, which would look lonely and out of scale. These are reproductions of typical Swedish pieces, with fluted carving and pretty pulls and escutcheons.

- The flat weave rugs framing the bed have a simple country grace. Plus, they balance the furniture, filling that extra floor space more delicately than a single, larger rug would.

- A little sparkle is essential for this look—the glass urn lamps add the perfect touch and they, too, are delicate, with sweet pleated shades carrying some brighter color up against the wall.

FINISHING TOUCHES
Offer guests a welcoming room

When friends and family come to stay, they appreciate a place to relax and be private. Whether your décor is lavish or spare, when you plan a guest room, apply the same principles used for your own refuge from the public part of your home, and add amenities that dispel any "living out of a suitcase" blues.

Simple décor is fine—guests won't feel as if they're sleeping in someone else's bed. If there is room, include a sofa, love seat, or pair of club chairs so that there's someplace other than the bed to sit and read or sip coffee. A bench to hold suitcases is a boon, too. Make sure there's a closet, even if it's small, and keep it empty of your own possessions. And nothing says "welcome" like a vase of fresh flowers. ▲

Keep it casual if that's what your house is—someone coming for a country weekend wants the getaway experience to extend to the guest room. Hang some interesting art—something with local connections or linked to a passion of yours. Be sure there's good reading light by the bed, and also a nightstand with room for books, a glass of water, and eyeglasses. Have extra blankets and pillows at hand and be sure to tell your guest where they're stored if you don't put them out. ▼

A room with character makes guests feel special. Period furnishings in a period home, pretty colors, and accessories that have stories to tell are all inviting. Anyone staying more than one night will appreciate a dresser for folded clothing and miscellaneous personal items. A mirror in the room is always welcome, especially if the bath is to be shared. If your home has nearby neighbors, is close to the street, or in a hot climate, window treatments that filter light during the day will help guests take their ease. ▼

DESIGNERS SPEAK

Even the nicest guest room may need some fine-tuning. Some experts remind us of amenities every guest will appreciate.

"A choice of pillows. There should always be a firm one, a soft one, and a hypoallergenic one. I'd love to say something glamorous—a bottle of Champagne—but if I don't have a good pillow, then I just don't sleep."

CAROLYNE ROEHM *Author*

"An iron and ironing board, a CD player with some good CDs to slip into it, a bathrobe—and a lock on the door."

ALEXANDRA STODDARD
Author and Interior Designer

"A TV. I am bereft without it."

PAULINE PITT *Interior Designer*

"Skirt or pants hangers and a luggage rack. I always travel with my own. When you have a guest room, the tendency is to be fussy about things, but sometimes it's the practical stuff that matters the most."

BARBARA MILO OHRBACH *Author*

"An alarm clock, but a cute one. I'm crazy about those little bitty ones from Braun—they're so chic and discreet. I have to confess, I would be tempted to steal it."

ELAINE GRIFFIN *Interior Designer*

"A good mirror, a clock I can read at night, and a reading light on each side of the bed—with a dimmer, a good narrow focus so you don't bother your partner, and an articulated arm."

PERI WOLFMAN *Author and Designer*

"Blackout curtains."

THOMAS BRITT
Interior Designer

"A warm, comfortable duvet. Not a particular brand, but a goose and feather down duvet. You never get enough blankets."

EVE ROBINSON *Interior Designer*

"Mystery books to add a little intrigue to the weekend, pads of paper and sharpened pencils by the bed, and peonies. You give me a guest room with all three and I'm in heaven."

ERIC COHLER
Interior Designer

Photography Credits

Pg. 2–3: Grey Crawford; **pg. 4–5** (left to right): Ken Hayden; John Ellis; Roger Davies; Tria Giovan; Jonn Coolidge; Pieter Estersohn; **Pg.6:** Eric Piasecki; **Pg.8:** Simon Upton; **Pg.11:** John Gould Bessler; **Pg.12:** Jonn Coolidge; **Pg.13:** Dana Gallagher; **Pg.14:** John Gould Bessler; **Pg.15:** Eric Piasecki; **Pg.16:** Don Freeman; **Pg.17:** Pieter Estersohn; **Pg.18:** Gordon Beall; **Pg.19:** Jeff McNamara; **Pg.20:** Tria Giovan; **Pg.21;** Anice Hoachlander/HD Photo; **Pg.22:** Simon Upton; **Pg.23:** Roger Davies; **Pg.24:** Karyn R. Millet; **Pg.25:** John Kernick; **Pg.26:** Kerri McCaffety; **Pg. 28–29** (clockwise from top right): Eric Piasecki; Kerri McCaffety; John Gould Bessler; John Kernick; **Pg.32:** John Ellis; **Pg.35:** Wayne Cable; **Pg. 36–37:** Gordon Beall; **Pg. 38–39:** John Ellis; Pages 40–41: Jonn Coolidge; **Pg.42:** Dominique Vorillon; **Pg.43:** Tim Street-Porter; **Pg.44:** Michel Arnaud; **Pg.45:** Grey Crawford; **Pg.46:** William Waldron; **Pg.47:** Grey Crawford; **Pg. 48–49:** Miki Duisterhof/Don Freeman; **Pg. 50–51:** Karyn R. Millet; **Pg.52:** Pieter Estersohn; **Pg.53:** Oberto Gili; **Pg.54:** Susan Gilmore; **Pg.55:** Pieter Estersohn; **Pg.56:** Wayne Cable; **Pg.57:** Simon Upton; **Pg.58:** J. Savage Gibson; **Pg.59:** Jeremy Samuelson; **Pg.60:** Jonn Coolidge; **Pg.61:** Dominique Vorillon; **Pg. 62–63:** Richard Felber; **Pg.64:** Eric Roth; **Pg.65:** Lisa Romerein; Pg.66: Grey Crawford; **Pg.67:** Eric Roth; **Pg.68:** Ken Hayden; **Pg.69:** Eric Piasecki; **Pg. 70–71:** Eric Roth; **Pg.72:** Pieter Estersohn; **Pg. 74–75** (clockwise from top right) Grey Crawford; Antoine Bootz; Andreas von Einsiedel; Gordon Beall; **Pg.78:** Tria Giovan; **Pg.81:** Dominique Vorillon; **Pg.82:** Dana Gallagher; **Pg.83:** Simon Upton; **Pg.84:** Dana Gallagher; **Pg.85:** Tria Giovan; **Pg.86:** Colleen Duffley; **Pg.87:** Simon Upton; **Pg.88:** John Gould Bessler; **Pg.89:** Jeremy Samuelson; **Pg.90:** Roger Davies; **Pg.91:** John Ellis; **Pg.92:** Dominique Vorillon; **Pg.93:** Dana Gallagher; **Pg.94:** Andreas von Einsiedel; **Pg.95:** Eric Piasecki; **Pg.96:** Victoria Pearson; **Pg.97:** Tria Giovan; **Pg.98:** Laura Moss; **Pg.99:** Tria Giovan; **Pg.100:** Grey Crawford; **Pg.101:** Simon Upton; **Pg.102:** Jack Thompson; **Pg.103:** Grey Crawford; **Pg.104:** Anice Hoachlander/HD Photo; **Pg. 106–107** (clockwise from top right): Roger Davies: Jack Thompson; Dana Gallagher; Anice Hoachlander/HD Photo; Grey Crawford; Simon Upton; **Pg.110:** Chuck Baker; **Pg.113:** Mick Hales; **Pg.114–115:** Ben Duggan; **Pg.116:** Joshua McHugh; **Pg.117:** Tria Giovan; **Pg.118:** Nathan Schroder; **Pg.119:** Jeremy Samuelson; **Pg.120:** William Waldron; **Pg.121:** William Waldron; **Pg.122:** Carlos Domenech; **Pg.123:** Tria Giovan; **Pg.124:** Pieter Estersohn; **Pg.125:** Mick Hales; **Pg.126:** Don Freeman; **Pg.127:** Firooz Zahedi; **Pg.128:** Roger Davies; **Pg.129:** Pieter Estersohn; **Pg.130:** John Gould Bessler; **Pg.131:** Lisa Romerein; **Pg. 132–133:** Eric Piasecki; **Pg.134:** Pieter Estersohn; **Pg. 136–137** (clockwise from top right): Mick Hales; Pieter Estersohn; Tria Giovan; Gordon Beall; John Ellis; William Waldron; **Pg.140:** Pieter Estersohn; **Pg.142:** Dana Gallagher; **Pg. 144–145:** Laura Moss; **Pg.89** (top and bottom): J. Savage Gibson; **Pg. 148–149:** Tria Giovan; **Pg.150:** Eric Piasecki; **Pg.151:** Lucas Allen; **Pg. 154–155:** Mick Hales; **Pg.152:** Pieter Estersohn; **Pg.153:** John M. Hall; **Pg. 156–157:** Eric Piasecki; **Pg.158:** Ellen McDermott; **Pg.159:** Grey Crawford; **Pg.160:** Grey Crawford; **Pg.161:** Pieter Estersohn; **Pg. 162–163:** Tria Giovan; **Pg.164:** Tria Giovan; **Pg.165:** Eric Piasecki; **Pg.166:** Roger Davies; **Pg.167:** Karyn R. Millet; **Pg.168:** Jonathan Wallen; **Pg.169:** Dana Gallagher; **Pg.170:** Gordon Beall; **Pg. 171:** Karyn R. Millet; **Pg. 172–173:** Francis Janisch; **Pg. 174–175:** Eric Roth; **Pg.176:** Karyn R. Millet; **Pg. 178–179** (clockwise from top right): Laura Moss; Grey Crawford; Tara Striano; Lucas Allen; Lucas Allen; Grey Crawford; **Pg.182:** Pieter Estersohn; **Pg.185:** Gordon Beall; **Pg. 186–187:** Karyn R. Millet; **Pg. 188–189:** Jonn Coolidge; **Pg.190:** Pieter Estersohn; **Pg.191:** Simon Upton; **Pg. 192–193:** Pieter Estersohn; **Pg.194:** Oberto Gili; **Pg.195:** Pieter Estersohn; **Pg.196:** Peter Murdock; **Pg.197:** Roger Davies; **Pg.198:** Jonn Coolidge; **Pg.199:** Grey Crawford; **Pg.200:** Pieter Estersohn; **Pg.201:** Jonn Coolidge; **Pg. 202–203:** John Gould Bessler; **Pg.204:** Pieter Estersohn; **Pg.205:** Antoine Bootz; **Pg.206:** John Gould Bessler; **Pg.207:** Tria Giovan; **Pg.208:** Eric Piasecki; **Pg.209:** Oberto Gili; **Pg.210:** Susan Gilmore; **Pg.211:** John Gould Bessler; **Pg.212:** William Waldron; **Pg.213:** Roger Davies; **Pg. 214–215:** Victoria Pearson; **Pg.216:** Victoria Pearson; **Pg.217:** Eric Boman; **Pg.218:** John Gould Bessler; **Pg. 220–221:** Gordon Beall; **Pg.224:** Laura Moss; **Pg.227:** Jonn Coolidge; **Pg.229:** Tria Giovan; **Pg. 230–231:** Tria Giovan; **Pg.232:** Victoria Pearson; **Pg.233:** Victoria Pearson; **Pg.234:** John Gould Bessler; **Pg.235:** John Gould Bessler; **Pg.236:** Jack Thompson; **Pg.237:** Pieter Estersohn; **Pg.238:** J. Savage Gibson; **Pg.239:** Simon Upton; **Pg.240:** Pieter Estersohn; **Pg.241:** Pieter Estersohn; **Pg.242:** Eric Roth; **Pg.243:** Peter Murdock; **Pg.244:** Don Freeman; **Pg.245:** Don Freeman; **Pg.246:** Roger Davies; **Pg.247:** Tria Giovan; **Pg.248:** Eric Piasecki; **Pg.249:** Tria Giovan; **Pg.250:** Don Freeman; **Pg.251:** Victoria Pearson; **Pg.252** (left and right): Laura Moss; **Page 253** (left and right): Grey Crawford; **Pg. 254–255:** Charles Maraia; **Pg.256:** Michael James O'Brien; **Pg.257:** Oberto Gili; **Pg. 258–259:** Gordon Beall; **Pg.260:** Oberto Gili; **Pg. 261:** Pieter Estersohn; **Pg. 262–263:** Eric Piasecki; **Pg.264:** Karyn R. Millet; **Pg. 266–267** (clockwise from top right): Tria Giovan; Michel Arnaud; Roger Davies.

Index